Suddenly there came a rushing, stampeding sound of many hoofs as cattle—they looked like millions to Laurel—came pounding around the curve, rushing straight at Laurel and her reluctant companion.

The animals snorted and plunged ahead, angrily dashing this way and that, clambering upon the running boards of the cars, and shying startled away. Laurel stood paralyzed with fear, every muscle frozen, as the beasts surged toward her. An instant more and she would be down beneath those awful trampling hoofs, crushed and bleeding—and that would be the end!

Then, just as she felt she was losing consciousness, strong arms caught her up, and she was lifted up the steep embankment. Now the screaming cattle, the roaring bulls, could not reach her, for the young man held her close in his arms. Her face was down on his breast, his back and shoulders taking the brunt of the crowding animals, his body protecting her at their every turn . . .

Crimson Mountain

LIVING BOOKS®
Tyndale House Publishers, Inc.
Wheaton, Illinois

This Tyndale House book
by Grace Livingston Hill
contains the complete text
of the original hardcover edition.
NOT ONE WORD
HAS BEEN OMITTED.

Library of Congress Catalog Card Number 88-50884
ISBN 0-8423-0454-1

Printed in the United States of America

99 98 97 96 95
11 10 9 8 7 6 5

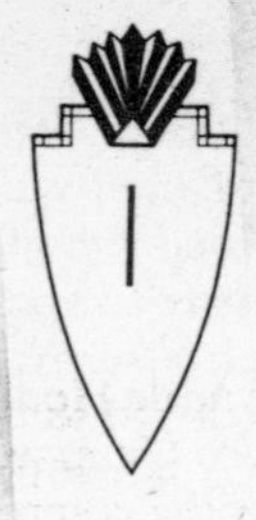

LAUREL Sheridan stood right in the way, as Phil Pilgrim rounded the curve and came rattling down the old road from the cow pasture, where he used sometimes to drive a few cattle to the Junction siding, long years ago when he was a mere boy living on his grandfather's farm.

She was a pretty girl with a halo of gold hair and big troubled blue eyes, and what was she doing there? This wasn't a regular road, just a cowpath to the Junction.

Phil hadn't wanted to take this road today. It held no pleasant memories. He had come here as a boy because there had been no other place for him to go when both father and mother died. His grandfather had sent for him, and they had lived there together, a couple of sorrowful hearts, one young, one old, never even getting well acquainted with one another, and both grieving silently for the ones who were gone. Then one morning his grandfather didn't wake up as usual at dawn, and when Phil returned from his early trip driving the cows to pasture, he found him dead in his bed with the first look of peace on the tired old face he had ever seen him wear.

The boy had walked down the mountain, got the undertaker and a couple of men who had been friendly to them, and they had buried the old man in the little hillside cemetery, across the road and a short distance down the mountain from the house. After that Phil locked the plain little home, went down to the village and got himself a job, also a place to work for his board and room. From that time on he began to save up till he could buy a simple stone to mark his grandfather's resting place, a mate to the stone which his grandfather had put up above his grandmother's grave.

It was to visit that simple little burying ground, to make sure his orders had been carried out about the stone, that Phil Pilgrim had taken that road that day. Of course it was a rough road, scarcely more than a cow-path in some places, but it passed both the old home and the cemetery. He wanted to stop a moment at the old house and look it over carefully, for he had received a letter the day before saying that the government was planning to build a munitions plant in that neighborhood and wanted to buy his land. He wanted to be sure whether he should sell it all or perhaps retain the house and a bit of land to rent. But it had been a sad pilgrimage and only brought back desolate days when it had seemed to him that life was nothing but a burden, young though he was.

He did not linger long after his investigations were over, and with lifted hat as he passed the little plot of ground at the edge of the road with its two white stones that gleamed side by side, he drove on down the mountain rapidly, glad to be away again out into a world that was not shrouded in sorrow.

Phil brushed his hand across his forehead and eyes and drew a deep sigh. He was bidding a final good-by to that sad youthful part of his life.

True, he had been out and away from it for a number

of years now. He had worked his way through high school, working Saturdays and after school in a filling station. Later he had won a scholarship to college, and had been a hard student there. Now he was through and had the coveted diploma that had been his goal for his dead mother's sake. And now suddenly the world had gone mad with war! So, he had taken the next step that duty demanded of him and enlisted. Life didn't look any too bright, anyway, even now when he had finished doing what he had been striving for so long. He hadn't had time for friends, or relaxation, except a little dash of athletics now and then when he had found that he could make his ability to run and swim into a source of more revenue.

But now all that was over. He was a soldier. He was wearing a uniform. He was going into a new life. And if, as some of them said, the next scene would be battle, with maybe death ahead, well, what of it? Would it be any worse than all the other changes that had come into his empty hard-working young life? Would there perhaps be Heaven, as his mother had always believed, where all the hard things would be over, and joy ahead forever? Well, it might be! But there must be surely some conditions to that, and he had never learned the conditions. If his mother had lived she might have taught him. Perhaps she had tried, but she was so sorrowful during those last days after his father was gone, and she was so ill and weak! Well, if there was a way out of this maze he would find it if he could, and work his way through, as he had worked it through other hard things. How he had gone out at night alone and practiced running, and in the dark, swimming, when his hard day's work was over! Oh, of course that had been good for him, too, keeping him in fine trim physically in spite of his plodding days, and nights of study and hard work. Yes, he would find a way through!

He wasn't looking forward eagerly to war, yet he must take it as he had taken all the rest, a way to attain on earth, or to reach Heaven if there was a Heaven.

He drew a deep heavy sigh.

Thoughts like these were unprofitable. He must get on. There were people in the village he must see. His old employer, a grim silent man, but he had been kindly at the end, and even allowed a small bonus on the last few months' work. He wanted to thank him for that kindliness. Then there was a small bank account he must look after. A professor in the high school to thank, who had given good advice, and helped him to understand some of the difficulties that might have hindered him. He must not forget any who had been his friends. They might have forgotten him by this time, doubtless had, for the months had been long and there were many boys coming and going about the village. But still he would feel better to have hunted them all out and thanked them for their kindliness.

A flight of purple grackles soared across the sky and dropped their bright iridescent blackness down among the autumn trees. They scattered on the ground searching for favorite food, filling the air with their strange fall sounds, those sounds that make summer seem so definitely a thing of the past, and the autumn sunshine only a passing gesture. Phil turned his eyes to the scene he was passing, and remembered days when he had wandered alone wishing for things that never came. There was a great flat stone by the roadside. He had sat there the morning he got the thorn in his foot, and tried to extract it. There was the big tree whose gnarled roots had made an arm chair where he came to study now and then, when he had some hard task to master. It was cushioned with velvet moss. Sometimes when he had been sitting there for a while he would get the idea that maybe in the future something nice would happen to him and then he could forget all the gloom and drabness of his life and be really happy. Yes? He had actually believed that. And look now, what was happening! Just out of college! No job, no special friends, no opportunity to forge into things and do something really worth while. War ahead! *Just war!* Life in a training camp! It hadn't been very exciting so far. And then what? Nothing to get excited or happy about. *Joy?* Maybe there wasn't any such thing as joy in this earth anyway, although he had always fancied that he saw other people having it.

Well, he mustn't get morbid. It certainly hadn't been a cheerful thing to come to his grandfather's old farm and the little cemetery. Still he had to come and see that everything was all right before he went back into camp and would no longer be able to order his life as he pleased. He had to be sure he wanted to sell.

Then with another deep sigh he swung his car around the curve of the hill, jolting along over the stony way, and there, right ahead of him, was a car standing with its hood open, and a girl in front of it, looking anxiously toward him. Fool girl getting in his way! He almost ran over her! Why did girls always have to get in the way? This was no road for a girl to be on anyway, a cattle path! How did she get here?

He ground on his brakes and came to an abrupt halt before her.

"I beg your pardon," he said politely. "Are you having engine trouble?"

"Yes, but I don't know what it is." The girl lifted her very blue eyes apologetically and instantly he wondered where he had seen those eyes before. Yet of course that was absurd. He didn't have much to do with girls, and especially not out here in the country. He never had had anything to do with girls, even in school, when he lived on Crimson Mountain. He was too busy studying and working. It must be something in his subconscious memory that was brought to him by the look in that girl's eyes.

These thoughts were vaguely passing through his mind as he sprang annoyedly from his car and went to investigate the other one. What a nuisance it was to be interrupted at this point in his journey, when he had only just so much time, and quite a good many things he wanted to do before he went on his way back to camp to meet whatever was about to be the next scene in his life.

Laurel Sheridan had turned from the highway several miles back into a wooded road that she *thought* was the short cut around the high hill that was familiarly known in that vicinity as Crimson Mountain because of its gorgeous color in the autumn. But Laurel did not choose that road for its beauty, although it was glowing and lovely. She was in a hurry. She was going to be late for an appointment and she was worried. She *thought* she remembered that this road was supposed to be the short cut to Carrollton. But it didn't seem to be so short. It certainly was farther than she remembered. *Could* she have made a mistake? It wasn't a very good road either, but she had come so far now she couldn't turn back. Oh, this *must* be right.

So, frantically she stepped on the gas, and mounted the hill, surprised at the sharp turn to the right that the road took when it ought to have turned left. She glanced at the clock in the car, calculating whether she could possibly get to that high school before it was entirely too late for her purpose.

She was two thirds of the way up the hill, and beginning to count the distance ahead, and discount time, when suddenly her car began to buck like a balky horse, and then it stopped dead!

She cast an annoyed glance at her dial. She couldn't be out of gas, could she? Horrors! With no filling station probably till she got to the foot of the mountain on the other side. She seemed to be all turned around. Which way *was* Carrollton, anyway? She certainly must have taken a wrong turn somewhere. Oh, it couldn't be her gas was out! And she was still going up. Oh, if she could only make the top of the hill, perhaps she could coast down safely and make a filling station. In vain she tried to start the car again, yet the dial showed a little gas. What a fool she had been to take this road, with no place to get help if she had trouble. This couldn't be the old short cut across Crimson Mountain. She hadn't had any doubt when she turned into the dirt road. It had seemed just as she remembered it, but now as she gave a quick look around somehow it didn't seem so familiar. She *must* have made a mistake. She tried to think back to the days of her little girlhood when her class had been brought into the woods for a picnic one day. What a happy time they had had, and how she had always looked wistfully toward that dirt road into which their cars had turned that day to bring them to the lovely woods on the top of Old Crimson. The look of that rough dirt road had always held a charm for her all that next winter after the picnic, whenever they drove down the highway. To tell the truth that was the main reason why she had turned into it today, although she *had* heard it was a shorter way, and she *was* in a hurry. After all, it was nearly five years since she had been in this region, and there might have been two roads. She had passed one about a quarter of a mile before she reached this one. But it had seemed to her too fine a road to lead to the old picnic place. She was positive that the picnic road of old had been a dirt road, and that first road had been macadam. But of course it might have been improved since early days. Well, what should she do now? If she could only get her engine going perhaps she could turn around and go back. Take that other road. Wouldn't that be best?

But try as she would she could not make her engine speak, and she drew an impatient sigh as she got out of her car and walked to the front. She was afraid of that hood. She had never succeeded in getting it open. The car had always been kept in order for her by the man at the garage and there was no one but herself to depend upon. She hadn't an idea what she was going to do when she got the hood open, but that was what all men did first when anything was the matter with a car—they opened the hood. So she struggled to open it and throw it back nonchalantly as she had seen the men in the filling stations do. But struggle as she might that hood refused to open. Till suddenly the handle she held gave a lurch and up it came! At least it came up about eight inches and then lurched back again and seemed to settle down harder than ever.

But Laurel was not a girl to give up easily, and she was becoming more and more conscious of that school committee she had promised to meet, where she was going to apply for a job. So she went at the matter more vigorously this time, and finally managed to swing up that hood and anchor it. She cast a troubled glance inside that mysterious engine, but nothing came of it. She had never had experience in machinery of any sort, and none of those pipes and tubes and screws made sense to her. For the first time it occurred to her as strange that anyone could have thought out and made a thing so complicated; and that being made, it could manage to carry people around the country. Before this she had always taken cars for granted, and thought nothing about them.

And so, having walked all about that engine and studied each part carefully without getting any light, she straightened up and stood there, trying to think what she should do next. Was it thinkable that she could *walk* down to the village and send somebody back from a filling station or garage after her car? She hadn't the slightest idea how far it would be, if indeed she was on the right road to Carrollton.

Then suddenly she heard the sound of a swiftly coming car. It was up around that curve ahead. She cast a quick anxious glance at the road. It seemed so narrow, and her car was right in the middle. There was a deep gully at one side and a steep embankment edged by thick woods on the other.

And then Phil Pilgrim's car came sweeping around the curve straight at her, and she stood petrified, her big blue eyes wide and startled.

He stopped just before he reached her.

Phil Pilgrim went over to the car and studied it a minute, swung himself in behind the wheel and tried out various parts of its mechanism with no result, swung out to the ground again and back to the engine, stooping to get a better view. Then he straightened up, looked at the girl, and said in a crisp reproachful tone as if it was entirely her fault:

"Your generator's shot."

"Oh!" said Laurel meekly. "Just what does that mean? What do I have to do?"

"Well, it means you'll have to have a new generator," he said with a grim smile. "What are you doing here anyway? This isn't a road. It's only a cattle path." He wanted her to understand that it was none of his affair. He had business in other directions.

"Oh!" she said again breathlessly. "I didn't know. Well, would there be some place near here where I could telephone for one?"

His smile became a half grin, or was there a shade of almost contempt in his tone as he answered?

"Well, not exactly!" He said it crisply. "They haven't established public telephone service yet on this highway."

"Oh, of course not," said Laurel with a timid little apologetic smile. "I ought to have known better of course. You see I thought this was a shortcut to Carrollton. I must have made a mistake somewhere. But at least I can walk down to the highway, can't I? It can't be so far away. Or, is it?"

There was an appeal in her voice and her eyes that made Phil Pilgrim ashamed.

"Oh, I guess it won't come to that," he said gruffly. He would have to take her to the town of course, and that would make no end of delay for him. What a nuisance that would be! He half wished he had not come up to Crimson himself, this afternoon, but then, what would the girl have done if he hadn't? He wasn't a youth who had practiced looking after himself and his own interests first. His mother had taught him courtesy and gentlemanliness before she left him in this world alone.

Then suddenly into the midst of his perplexity, and the strained silence that his words had brought, came a rushing, stampeding sound of many hoofs, pounding along the road around which young Pilgrim had just come. And then appearing as suddenly as he had done, came cattle. They looked to Laurel like millions, as their brown faces and wild excited eyes surmounted by terrifying horns showed around the curve and pelted straight at her.

She cried out in terror and then she was speechless with horror as the frightened creatures came on, headed by two angry bulls escaped from their keepers, who were now running wildly in pursuit and shouting to them, but only adding to the confusion.

It was not a large herd, and would not have been unmanageable perhaps if it had not been for those two unexpected cars, and the man and girl. But now the animals snorted and plunged ahead, climbing up and over one another, angrily dashing this way and that, clambering upon the running boards of the cars, and shying startled away. The girl stood paralyzed with fear, her brain refusing to act, every muscle frozen. An instant more and she felt she would be down beneath those awful trampling hoofs, crushed and bleeding, and that would be the end!

Then just as she felt that she was losing consciousness, and knew it would be impossible either to run, or withstand the onslaught that was coming, strong arms behind her caught her up, away above that horde. With what seemed like superhuman strength, she was lifted up the steep embankment, above where the two cars stood.

Though barely higher than the struggling creatures she no longer felt their hot breath on her face, and even the screaming of the cattle, the roaring of the bulls, seemed below her.

And yet the creatures were still there, struggling past in one wild melee. She could dimly feel their crowding, pushing forms jostling now and again, when one of them struggled up the bank. But they could not reach her, for the young man held her close in his arms. Her face was down on his breast, his back and shoulders were taking the brunt of the crowding animals, his body protecting her at their every turn.

Gradually she came to herself and realized these things, feeling strangely safe there in the midst of all the confusion.

It seemed an eternity, while those puffing snorting frightened steers were floundering frantically past them. The young man held his place on that steep hillside, now and then sliding, shoved aside and almost falling, yet holding his footing, with Laurel in his arms. Yet in reality it was only a very short time, for the animals were not many, and the two men and three boys who were attending them were doing their best to get them back to the road, and to corral the angry bulls. The attendants did not seem even to notice the man and the frightened girl on the bank above the cars. Or if they saw them they had no time to look at them and wonder. They were just a part of the obstacles that had caused the confusion. Fool people who came into a cattle road where they had no right to be! If they got frightened or hurt it was their own fault. There was a sign at both ends of this road, and surely anybody in this age of the world could read. And if this was an accident it wasn't *their* accident and they had no time to stop. It was their business to prevent an accident of their own. And so they presently passed on.

It seemed hardly credible that the wild teeming creatures were gone, and they two were alone at last. Then suddenly Laurel realized that she was in the arms of a strange young man! She opened frightened eyes almost afraid to break this blessed silence that had left them there together, alive and safe.

Pilgrim looked down at her with troubled eyes.

"Are you all right?" He asked in a low tone, almost as if those departed steers were enemies who might hear and return.

The touch of his arms about her, the tone of his voice, thrilled Laurel as nothing had ever done before, but the only reply she seemed able to make was a trembling nod. She was not a girl given to thrills, or to tears, but suddenly she felt tears coming, and knew they would greatly complicate the scene. She must not let them come. He would think she was a fool. She closed her eyes quickly to drive them back and two great tears rolled out and down her cheeks.

"You are hurt!" he charged anxiously. "Did one of

those beasts touch you? Did their horns reach you anywhere? I tried hard to cover you. Where are you hurt?"

"No, no, I am not hurt," she protested quickly, struggling to rise. "I was only frightened and kind of shaken up. It is silly of course. But you were wonderful. You saved my life! You can put me down now. I'm quite all right!"

"That's good," said Pilgrim. "I'm *glad.* But I guess we won't let you down on this steep hillside. Hark! What was that?"

He lifted his head alertly and looked back toward the curve around which the cattle had come so suddenly. Then his face grew grave.

"We must get out of here before another bunch of cattle comes," he said sternly. "There are two more farmers up here where they raise a few cows, and when one of the three gets a bunch ready to ship, the other two try to send some at the same time. This is the cattle path straight down to the railroad siding at the Junction. They have probably arranged to have the four o'clock train stop and take on their stock. That's the way it used to be when I lived up this way. Are you quite sure you are all right?"

He gave her another keen look.

Then without giving her opportunity to answer, he strode firmly down to the road, Laurel still in his arms, gave one quick glance behind and ahead, and put her in the seat of his own car.

WE'LL have to get off this road before any more steers come," said Pilgrim anxiously as he swung in behind the wheel of this car, slammed the door shut, and began to back and cut, back and cut, to turn around in the narrow road. "You won't mind riding to the village in my old roadster?"

"Of course not," said Laurel, struggling for her normal self-control. "You've been wonderfully kind. I don't know what I should have done if you hadn't come along. I wouldn't have been here long enough to do anything. Those creatures would likely have trampled me to death. I was simply petrified! I couldn't have moved an inch. You saved my life!"

He gave her a quick look.

"I'm glad I was here!" he said crisply. "I almost didn't come this way."

"God must have sent you," said Laurel reverently.

"Maybe," he said thoughtfully. "I've never had much to do with God!"

"Neither have I," said Laurel soberly, her eyes very thoughtful. "But I've heard people say He cares."

"Could be," said the young man cryptically. "But I've never seen reason in my life to think He cared. Still, if He were going to care for anybody, I should think He might care for you!"

Suddenly he lifted his head alertly.

"Hark! There's that sound again! I thought I heard the voice of one of Hunsicker's men. There'll be more animals coming or I'll miss my guess. You don't mind if I go some, do you? I think we maybe can beat 'em to it. We'd better get by before they start out from the next farm."

His face set grimly. The girl cast a frightened glance at him, gripping the cushion of the seat tensely, her heart beating wildly again.

They fairly flew up the long hill, bordered on the one hand now by a rough wall of field stone, piled up without cement, and on the other hand by a deep gully. She could see a shackly wooden gate ahead flanked by a great red barn so weathered that it blended with the autumn trees that stood about it, and out of its wide door were coming more steers! Laurel caught her breath involuntarily, and Pilgrim turned and flashed a quick reassuring smile as they flew on.

"Don't worry," he said. "We're going to make it. They haven't started yet. I'll take care of you."

There was something about his quiet assurance that calmed her fears.

As they rushed past the old wooden gate now, Laurel could see the group of animals coming down toward the road from the old red barn. Though they were moving in a fairly quiet and orderly mass, the sight of their brown backs, their woolly brown heads, topped by that terrifying fringe of horns, was anything but comforting.

As they swept past the gate and onward, Pilgrim turned toward her.

"We're all right now," he said gently. "We've passed their gate, and they are going the other way so they can't catch up with us. There's only one more farm to pass, and we'll likely be able to miss any there. It might even be that they won't be sending any cattle down. They are not very successful cattle raisers. But anyway we'll get ahead of them, I'm sure."

So, silently they drove on, rushing over the rough cart road.

And then they came in sight of another little old farmhouse set almost sullenly back from the road. But there were no animals in sight. There wasn't even a dog around nor any chickens.

Laurel's tensity relaxed and she sat back more comfortably.

Pilgrim watched her furtively.

"You're not frightened any more," he said in a satisfied tone. "We've passed all the farms now. Those last people must have moved away, or died, or something. And now it won't be far to a garage where we can send someone back for your car. But look around. Isn't this a lovely spot? I always liked it here."

They had reached the top of the hill and were passing through the woods. Laurel exclaimed in delight over the beauty of the way. Pilgrim watched her as her face lighted up at each new turn.

"There's a thrush!" she said joyfully. "There isn't any bird song quite like that, is there? And I've been away from them so long they sound just wonderful to me."

"Yes," said Pilgrim a bit sadly. He was thinking that the last time he remembered hearing the thrushes sing was while they were burying his grandfather, the grandfather with whom he had lived so long, and whom he had known so little.

He gave another furtive look at the girl beside him.

Suddenly he spoke:

"Where have I seen you before? Did you ever live in Carrollton?"

Her face clouded sadly.

"Yes," she said, "I lived there when I was a little girl."

He looked at her sharply.

"I see," he said, "and I've seen you as a little girl, going about the town, or perhaps in school. And your eyes have stayed the same. It's your eyes that made me think I had seen you before."

Laurel laughed.

"That's strange," she said. "I've been thinking just that about *your* eyes. But I can't place you. You couldn't have been in school with me or I would have known your name, I am sure."

He looked at her gravely and shook his head.

"No, I'm too old for that. I must have finished high school before you entered, or at least in your first year. I was working in a filling station at least part time, long before you were in high school, I guess. Who are you, anyway? I'm sure I've seen you, though I may not have known your name. It couldn't possibly be Sheridan, could it?"

"Yes, I'm Laurel Sheridan."

"Sheridan! Langdon Sheridan's daughter?"

"Yes."

"And when you were a little child you used to drive down in your father's car when it came for gas and oil! You used to come with the chauffeur, and sit in the back seat with your doll or a book while I filled up your car."

"Oh!" said the girl. "Yes, that's right. And now I remember you. You were the one they called Phil! Isn't that right?"

"That's right," said the young man, and there was a certain grimness about the set of his lips and the firm line of his jaw.

Then after a pause he added:

"Yes, I was working in a filling station and you were living in a stone mansion on Bleecker Street, the daughter of the most important man in the town, heiress to a fortune! There wasn't any chance that we should have met even enough to have remembered one another. Though I do remember that little girl with the big blue eyes, the eyes that looked at me back there in the road when I almost ran into you. I couldn't place you at first, but I remembered those eyes."

"Yes, and I remember the nice boy that waited on us at the filling station, the boy they called Phil. And afterward I heard of a Phil Pilgrim who won the prizes at high school for his scholarship, and his marvelous feats in running and swimming. Were you that one? I only heard the talk about you when I was in high school. So you are the boy who was so noted a character in those days on the athletic field."

Pilgrim bowed assent.

"Yes, I went to college afterward, and that was a way to help along financially."

"Oh, of course. Why, how wonderful that I should meet you this way! How wonderful that you came along just when I was in such dire need!"

"It's kind of you to feel that way," said Pilgrim with a touch of aloofness in his voice. "I certainly am glad I was able to help you a little. It will make a pleasant incident to remember when I am overseas—or wherever they are sending me."

"Oh!" said Laurel in a small sorry voice. "Are you—to go overseas?"

"Oh, I don't know what they are going to do with me. That's not my lookout. But it will be all right, whatever it turns out to be. After all I haven't had such a fancy life thus far that I can make any kick at what's coming," and he turned a cool little grin toward her.

"Oh, I'm sorry," said Laurel. "But where did you

live in Carrollton? I don't remember that I ever heard."

"No, you wouldn't," said the young man with a sigh. "It wasn't in your region at all. In fact, if you're interested, we're going to pass the old farmhouse in about two minutes, where I lived alone with my grandfather for a good many years."

"We *are?*" said Laurel. "Yes, I *am* interested. I'd like to know all about you. You saved my life, you know, and of course I'm interested."

He turned another frank gaze on her.

"That's good of you," he said. "Well, there it is, up on the brow of the hill. Just an old farmhouse, and all run down now. Nobody's lived there since Grandfather and I were there."

Laurel turned troubled eyes on the bleak old farmhouse glooming there on the hillside, gloomy even among the gorgeous autumn foliage on the few big trees around it.

"Oh—is that really where you lived?" said the girl with a pitiful tone in her voice. "And—what became of your grandfather?" And then when she saw the look on the young man's face she wished she hadn't asked.

Phil Pilgrim took a deep breath and lifting his right hand from the wheel, pointed across and down the road to the two sad little white stones over there among the grass by the roadside.

"He is lying over there beside Grandmother," he said solemnly.

Laurel looked at the two small white stones gleaming there in that desolate field among the gay foliage of Crimson Mountain.

"Oh, I'm sorry," said the girl softly, and turned toward the young man, eyes bright with tears.

Phil Pilgrim gave her a grateful shadow of a smile and turned his head quickly away, looking off toward the mountains beyond his old home.

They drove on in silence for two or three minutes, the thoughts of each mingled with the story of the dreary home and the two white stones that marked a resting place.

Then all at once they swept around a group of trees and there below them lay the village, with a filling station half hidden at their feet down the road a half mile.

"There!" said the young man, pointing down. "There's our filling station. It won't be long now," and he tried to say it cheerfully.

"Well, I'm glad you will soon be relieved of responsibility on my behalf. I don't know how to express my gratitude."

"Don't try, please. It has been a pleasure."

Then a moment later a macadam road ambled up from the valley and crept away into a wide opening in the woods at the right, and Laurel exclaimed excitedly:

"Oh, but isn't that the road to the picnic grounds! That's the road I thought I was taking up from the other side."

"Yes, that's the road you *should* have taken, Miss Sheridan, if you came in on route thirty. This is the new stretch of road that used to be the short cut from route thirty. But I'm glad you didn't, for then I shouldn't have had the pleasure of rescuing you, and perhaps I would never have known anything of you except the memory of the little girl with the gold curls and the eyes! But you must have gone at least two miles out of your way."

Then he drove down with a sweep and into the road in front of the gasoline pumps, but Laurel had a sudden sinking feeling that she was never going to see him any more. Absurd of course! He was only a *stranger.* What difference did it make whether she ever saw him again or not? Three hours ago she had had no consciousness of his existence, and here she was feeling all gone because she thought she wouldn't see him any more. What a little idiot she was! It was all because she had been through such a shock. All those awful creatures practically climbing over her! She shuddered as she remembered it again, her fright, her horror! And then those arms! Lifting her high above the milling, snorting horde, holding her safe above it all. She never could forget it! Oh, he was no stranger now, and never could be! He had saved her life! And yet, he was going away! She wouldn't see him anymore!

She watched him as he swung out of the car and went to speak to the young proprietor of the garage. She saw the grave pleasant smile with which he greeted the man, who evidently recognized him and flashed an intelligent look as Phil Pilgrim went on to tell about the car up on Crimson Mountain, stalled, needing, he thought, something done to the generator. The gesture with which he pointed to another car standing near made it plain to Laurel as she watched. Yes, he was good-looking, and probably it was just as well that he was going away. Though she had never thought herself one to get her head turned by a handsome face, a courteous smile. But then, having had one's life saved, it was nice to have as her rescuer one with an attractive appearance, something pleasant to remember.

She finished this homily to herself as Phil came back to explain to her.

"He's sending a man up immediately after your car. I've told him just where to find it. If you'll give him the keys he'll tow the car down, and let you know what has to be done. Now, in the meantime, I don't suppose you want to just hang around here, do you? Haven't you some place you would like to go while you are waiting? I'll be glad to take you wherever you suggest. I've practically nothing to do till the midnight train comes in, when I have to meet a man who wants to see my farm. I'll be glad to see you through till your own car is seaworthy."

"Oh, thank you, but I couldn't think of troubling you further after all you have done for me. I'll be quite all right now. And I'm within walking distance of several people I know."

"You're not fit to walk," said Phil Pilgrim in his firm tone. "You don't realize how much you were shaken by that experience on the mountain. I'm sorry to have to force my company on you any longer, but I guess there's no way out, unless you can think of some friend you'd rather have take you places."

He smiled his engaging smile, and Laurel felt that breathless catch in her breath as she answered.

"Oh, no, there's no one I'd rather have take me. I just don't want to be any further nuisance to you."

"Well, so far you haven't been a nuisance. In fact you've helped to bring me out of an unpleasant situation that duty forced me into. I came here to look at my worthless property and see whether I should accept an offer I've had for it, or hold it till I get back from wherever I'm going. I also came to look at the family graves that belong to my care and see if they are getting the attention I had ordered. It wasn't a very cheerful errand. Having concluded it, there was time to be passed till I could meet my man, so if I can be of any further service it will relieve a tiresome monotony, and you will be doing me a favor. Where were you going when I met you on the mountain and your car balked?"

"Oh!" said Laurel with a startled look. "I was going in a great hurry to an appointment, but I guess it's away too late for that now." She lifted her hand and glanced anxiously at her wrist watch. "Well, maybe not. Perhaps I had better go and see if anybody is there yet. I wouldn't like them to think I hadn't kept my word. If you would be so good as to take me to the high school. I was to have met the board there an hour ago. They are probably gone now. But at least I could say I came as soon as I was able."

"Sure!" said Phil. "Have you there in two minutes. But surely you're not still in high school?" He gave her a mischievous grin.

She smiled appreciatively.

"No," she said, "nothing so good as that. I'm applying for a position as substitute, in place of a teacher who is very sick. You see that fabulous fortune you thought I was supposed to inherit vanished when my father died, and the 'stone mansion' was sold, so I am in search of a position to earn my living." She said it gaily, but there was a hint of sadness in her voice that made him look at her with a softened glance.

"Oh, I didn't know. Well, suppose we see what we can find out. There goes the wrecking truck. Now, your car ought to be brought back soon. I told him I'd be back within an hour to find out about it. Let's go!" His old car whizzed out into the highway rushing along like one who knew the way, and Laurel sat still wondering about it all. She ought to be thanking him again, but somehow it didn't seem possible to get her gratitude across to him. He just didn't take it. He was doing things as a matter of course, as if that was his business in life, just the way she remembered he used to clean the windshield of her father's car, and check the water and oil, sort of impersonally. It seemed to express a fineness of breeding that one would not look for in a man who was doing a menial task. It was as if to him no task was menial.

As she rode along by his side now she had no sense that he was socially her inferior. In fact if a Sheridan had *ever* had an overweening sense of class distinction, it was thoroughly purged out of Laurel now by the fire of sorrow.

As she considered the memory of the grim little farmhouse on the side of Crimson Mountain, sitting amid all the sadness of the past, it took on a kind of sacred dignity, like one who might have worn princely robes at some time long gone by, but now sat in dull habiliments of mourning.

THEY drew up presently in front of the high school.

"They'll be meeting in the principal's office, I suppose, if they are still here," he said. "Would you like me to go in and find out?"

"Oh, no, I'd better run in myself, and then if they are still there I can save them a little time by going right in. Besides, I mustn't take any more of your time."

"Please don't say that," he smiled. "My time is yours until I've seen you in possession of your car again. I'm really not in a hurry."

She looked into his frank eyes and quietly accepted his planning.

"That's very good of you," she said. "I thank you. I'll be as quick as possible."

"All right. I'll wait a few minutes now, in case they have left. And if the hour is up before you come, I'll run across to the drugstore and telephone the garage."

She smiled and hurried up the walk into the school.

A moment later he saw her shadow as she crossed the front window in the principal's office, and took a seat where he could see her.

He sat there in the car going over the strange events of the afternoon and trying to work them out clearly and define this queer feeling of exultation that seemed to dominate him, unlike any emotional stirring that had ever come to him before.

"Silly!" he said to himself. "She's not in your class! Do all you can for her, and then get on your way! Your paths will not cross again."

But still he sat and went over what had happened, remembering her tones of voice, the way she had lifted her eyes to look at him, the exquisite turn of cheek and lip and chin, the very likeness of her childish self when she used to come with the chauffeur, and her doll. How strange life was! Why had she crossed his path just now when he was likely going away from this part of the world entirely? He would probably never see her again in this life after today. And she was the first young woman who had ever won his thoughts away from the path he had set himself to walk.

He had thought he was immune to the wiles of girls. He had kept his own way through college, had declined the few invitations that came to him, had been too busy to step aside into the world. Furthermore he had lived too close to Nature and the great out-of-doors to admire the artificiality of most worldly girls. He had merely glanced past them and escaped from all but passing contact.

But this girl was different. Or else perhaps he hadn't looked at the others closely enough to see any beauty in them. He had never been quite so near to any girl before, since his mother died. He thrilled at the thought of Laurel in his arms. There hadn't been time to think much about it while it was happening, but to hold that light helpless figure had been like holding something very precious, preserving it from danger, and the soft pressure of her head against his shoulder, the touch of her hair against his face lingered in his thoughts as a costly perfume might that had touched his garments. Just to draw his breath and feel the sweetness over again gave him a new and exquisite pleasure that he had never before dreamed there might be in the world.

Of course she was not for him. She belonged to a world into which he could not enter. A world of fashion and culture in which he was utterly unfitted to live. A costly world where only the wealthy could enter with ease. Of course she might say her father's fortune was gone, but she had been brought up under its privileges. She had never had to struggle for a bare existence, and would not understand what his struggling life had been. She was not for him!

And yet he would always be glad that he had been privileged to hold her close for those moments of danger. He would never forget the thrill of his very soul as he felt that soft hair on his cheek. He considered it most reverently, and marveled at the power that memory had over his spirit. Or was it just over his senses?

Oh, this was madness. He must snap out of it quickly!

He passed a quick hand across his forehead impatiently, firmly over the cheek where her soft cloud of hair seemed still to linger, shook his head as if to shake the dreams out of his mind, and looked at his watch. There was plenty of time to go over to that drugstore across the road and make three or four phone calls that would practically cover the matter of the errands he had not been able to work in that afternoon. That would leave him free to do anything for the girl that was needful without her having to know that she was hindering him. Indeed those errands were none of them important. He had only planned them because he had this time off, and he wanted to kid himself into feeling that he had some home interests. Though of course it wouldn't matter to a soul in Carrollton whether he called them up or not. But just to get his thoughts back into sensible every day normal channels he swung himself out of the car, snapped its door shut behind him, and strode across to the drugstore, at once immersing himself in a study of the telephone book.

But he found he was only half-heartedly interested now. Instead of eagerly accepting the invitations that these former associates of his offered, to come to dinner, or spend the evening, he found no inclination whatever in his heart for any such plans.

"Thank you, I don't believe that will be possible this trip," he told them all. "If I find I can get done what I am doing and can drop around for a few minutes later I'll call you up."

He turned away from the telephone half disgusted with himself. What did he have in the back of his mind that he did not want to go to his former friends? If it had anything to do with the girl into whose attention he had been thrust today he had better cut it out. Oh, of course, it was just possible that when she came out of the schoolhouse there might be some urgent errand she ought to go on for which he would have to offer his services. And it was true that he should in courtesy keep the way clear to help a lady in distress.

A glance through the window showed that Miss Sheridan had not yet come out of the schoolhouse, and his watch showed the hour was up when he was to call the garage. He turned back to the telephone.

"Hello! Is this Mark? This is Pilgrim speaking. Have you got the car back? What seems to be the trouble? Was I right?"

It wasn't a long conversation, but a rather grave one.

"You can't do any better than that? The girl is in a hurry to get her car. You're sure you haven't the necessary parts? Well, could I help by running in town to get anything? Oh, Chester has gone over to Granby, you say? And if he succeeds in getting what you need can you fix it tonight? Well, about what time tomorrow? I see. Well, I'll tell her, and meanwhile do your best, and we'll drop around there in a little while and see how you are making out."

He went back to his car, a kind of pleasant elation filling him in spite of his common sense.

He took his seat in the car, but his attention was toward the window where Laurel had been sitting before he went across the road to telephone. She had disappeared from it now.

While he sat watching the high school door for her appearance his mind was busy thinking out possibilities. No, not really possibilities, just fantastic dreams.

Where would she be going for dinner? Could he by any stretch of imagination ask her to go with him? Of course not. A former filling station assistant taking a multi-millionaire's daughter to dinner! It was not to be even thought of.

He drew a deep breath and threw his chin up in that gesture of challenge that was significant of his own quiet pride.

Suddenly she was coming out the door, poising an instant on the top step, looking toward the car, then hurrying down as lithely and gaily as a young scholar slipping out for recess. Without his knowledge Phil's sternness went into a welcoming smile.

And Laurel's face was wreathed in smiles too.

"I'm sorry I kept you waiting so long," she said as she stepped into the car, accepting Pilgrim's courteous help. "I hadn't an idea it was going to take so long or I would have told you to go on and forget about me."

"Yes?" he said with a grin. "You're not so easy to forget, my lady. And remember, we still have business to transact."

"Business?" said Laurel lifting questioning eyes to his.

"Your car," he reminded.

"Oh, yes, of course," said the girl in chagrin. "But I should have told you not to bother any further about that. You know, really I'm not a baby, and if I'm going to teach school and earn my own living I've got to learn to look after my own car, and all my other affairs."

"Yes?" said Pilgrim with a little tinge of his habitual gravity edging his grin. "But not when there's a gentleman near to help. At least I hope I can count as a gentleman."

She gave him a swift questioning look. Had she somehow hurt him?

"Oh—why, *of course,*" she said heartily. "I don't think I ever saw one with more courtesy. You've been perfectly marvelous. But I certainly am ashamed to have taken advantage of your courtesy all this time. And I mustn't do it any longer. If you'll just take me back to that garage we'll call it a day and—you can go on your way."

Her voice trembled the least little bit as she said it, and she cast a frightened look up at him, trying to smile quite calmly.

He read all that in his one glance at her face, and his own took on a tenderer light.

"Say, now, look here! Why can't you give up that 'perfectly marvelous' way of looking at this thing, and just for the time being pretend that we are old friends? I'll promise you I'll never take advantage of you afterwards on account of it."

She gave him a quick almost indignant look.

"Of course not!" she said definitely. "Even though we're practically strangers, I would *know* that as well as if I had known you for years."

"Thank you," he said pleasantly. "But you forget. We're not strangers. Not even practically. We *are* old friends, at least for the convenience of the day. Childhood friends, or, if you prefer, school friends. We might compromise on that, although I do look a little old to have been a contemporary of yours in school."

"I don't think you do," said Laurel quickly. "When people are grown up no one stops to count the years between them. And it's a woman's business to keep young-looking of course, especially if she has to earn her living." She gave him a merry little twinkle and pushed her hair back from her forehead.

"Oh, by the way," said Pilgrim, "how did you make out?"

"Why, I made out very well when they finally got around to me," she said. "They must have been somewhat peeved that I wasn't there at the beginning of the session, or else that's their usual way of keeping applicants on nettles until they have had opportunity to study them carefully. At any rate, after they had given me a chair they practically ignored me until they had canvassed a number of unimportant matters, like what they were going to do with one named Jimmy; and whether they should give up a certain kind of soap for cleaning that they have bought for years, in favor of a new kind which claims to do the work more cheaply; and whether they should allow any students to help in the cafeteria, or require the matron in charge to do all the work. But after due time had passed, and all the questions of the universe had been settled, they put me through a rigid questionnaire and then hired me. I am to begin Monday."

"That's good, if that's what you really want," said the young man, looking at her keenly as if he would search out her real feelings in the matter.

"Well, I do," said the girl thoughtfully, and not very cheerfully. "I'm not so strong on Carrollton, but if I don't get started somewhere I'll never get anywhere. But what did the man say about my car? Have you telephoned?"

"Yes. It was generator trouble as I thought, and in consequence a fuse blown. He says he can't possibly get it fixed for you before some time tomorrow morning. How is that going to affect your plans? Have you a place to stay here all night, or would you like me to drive you to the city?"

"Oh, I couldn't possibly let you do that," she said in dismay. "I'll have to find a place to stay. Eventually I'm *staying* of course. But I'm not sure where yet. Didn't there used to be a hotel in Carrollton?"

"Yes, but it's not a very possible solution for you," said Pilgrim. "It's rather tough. It isn't a place your father would have wanted you to stay. But there must be some tourist place. We'll see."

"I know," said Laurel. "There used to be a dear lady who lived not far from our old home, in a little cottage. Perhaps she would rent me a room. At least she would take me in for the night until I can have a chance to look around for the right place for the winter. That is, if she is still living. I haven't heard anything about her for years. She is Mrs. Browning. Did you know her?"

"Did she have a crippled daughter, and did she live in that little white cottage on Maple Street, with the ivy all over the porch and red geraniums growing along the walk?"

"Why yes, that's the place! Did you know her?"

"No, I didn't exactly know her, but I used to carry eggs and chickens down to her from Hunsicker's farm when I was a kid. She was nice smiling lady, and sometimes gave me a dime over price."

"Yes, she was like that. Well, I'll try her. Perhaps I could telephone her from the garage."

"Yes, that would be a good idea," said the young man, with a sudden dismayed feeling that he was about to lose contact with this girl, who had seemed for a few minutes as if she belonged to him.

So when they reached the garage Phil Pilgrim went with Mark to look at the car, and Laurel went to the telephone. But Laurel came back a few minutes later with dismay in her face.

"She's gone out west to live with her married daughter," she said. "Her crippled daughter died, and she was all alone. She's been gone a couple of years."

"Say, that's tough luck!" said Pilgrim. "But don't worry. We'll find something. Mark, how about Mrs. Topham? Is she still keeping boarders? Not that she's so hot as a cook," he explained to Laurel, "but she's good and respectable."

"No," said Mark flinging down the big wrench with which he was working, and picking up another tool. "M's. Topham was taken to a sanitarium two months ago, and her married daughter doesn't take boarders. But if the lady wants a good place whyn't ya take her ta the new tea room? It's over on Houston Road, and they have swell meals there. They've got a few rooms too, I hear, an' I think the lady would like it there."

"Thank you," said Laurel. "That sounds good to me."

"All right," said Pilgrim. "Let's go and investigate. Are there any things in your car you want to take along, in case you find a place to stay, Miss Sheridan?"

"Oh, yes, my little overnight bag. It's in the back of the car. The small key in the case fits it."

Pilgrim unlocked the compartment and brought the bag.

"Now," he said to the garage man, "Mark, how about that generator? You said Chester couldn't get one in Granby. Have you telephoned the city about it yet?"

"Sure thing," said Mark importantly. "Yes, they have it and they're putting it on the five-ten train for me. If all goes well you'll have your car the first thing in the morning, lady, or a least before noon, unless something more turns up. But I've looked the car all over, and I don't see anything else the matter."

"Well, that will be all right, I guess, but I'll have to telephone again, I'm afraid, Mr. Pilgrim." She turned apologetically to Phil. "I had an engagement this evening that I forgot all about, and I'll have to call it off. I won't be a minute, if you don't mind waiting."

Phil Pilgrim stood just outside the window that sheltered the telephone and he couldn't help hearing the conversation.

"Hello, is that you, Adrian? Yes, this is Laurel. Why, I'm sorry, Adrian, I can't go with you tonight. I had a little car trouble and have to wait for repairs. No, nothing serious. Something went wrong with the generator, and I had to wait for the parts to come. What? You'll come after me? No indeed, Adrian. I couldn't think of letting you do that. It's much too far for you to make it and get back in time for your other guests, and it would throw all your plans out. I'm very sorry to disappoint you but it isn't anything I could help. Of course I should have telephoned you sooner, but I didn't know till just now that I won't be able to get my car before morning. No, it's quite impossible, Adrian . . . Oh yes, I'll be all right. I have friends here. I'm sorry to disappoint you. When? Why yes, I may be able to see you Saturday evening if you should happen to be around. That is, I *think* I'll be at home then, but I can't be sure. I could telephone if I get back. Sorry, Adrian, but I know you'll understand how it is. Good-by!"

Laurel came out of the little glass room with a smile. She wasn't feeling badly at missing her date! Or *was* she? Maybe she was smiling at hearing a beloved voice. How could he tell? Pilgrim wished he hadn't overheard the conversation. He wished this hadn't happened just now. Somehow it dimmed the pleasure that he had been anticipating in the small expedition upon which they were about to embark. Of course she would have men friends. She had been going somewhere with one of them tonight.

But Laurel got into the Pilgrim car quite happily. Her friend Adrian had evidently not been happy over the canceling of their engagement, and had been quite insistent that he would come after her, but she reflected contentedly that she had got away with the interview without telling him just where she was, or giving him any clue to find her. And now he couldn't possibly trace her and come after her even if he tried.

And he probably would try. Adrian Faber was that way. He always tried everything there was to try to carry out his point.

To tell the truth she had come away from the city in haste and without leaving details of her whereabouts partly because she had felt it was essential that she should be by herself and think a few things through to their finish, without the influence of any of her friends to distract her attention, especially the insistent friends who would go to the length of trying to make her marry them to prevent her going away. And she was not at all sure that she wanted to marry *any*one. At least not now.

Also the events of the afternoon had put a new phase on life and made her feel that there was much to be understood and settled before she was ready to consider marriage with anybody.

So Laurel came back to the examination of her car with a lighter heart, having rid herself of an obligation which had troubled her more or less all day, because she had literally dreaded this evening's engagement, and had had only half an intention of returning in time to keep it anyway.

"Well, it all depends on whether the new part comes down on the five-ten train or not," said Pilgrim as she came toward him smiling.

"Yes?" said Laurel. "And—if the part *doesn't* come, then what?"

"Well, we'll wait till the train comes in, and if it isn't on the train, *somebody* is driving after it. Don't worry. I think we'll manage it somehow."

"Oh, but *you mustn't!"* said Laurel with instant trouble in her eyes. "You've done so much already. You *can't* drive sixty-five miles after a part for my car! I've practically used up half a day of your precious leave, and I simply won't accept any more services. There must be someone I could pay to go after it. Or, wait! I could go back to the city on the train myself. There is an evening train. I looked up trains before I ventured over here, because I didn't want to put myself permanently where there wouldn't be good train service any time I needed it. Then I could leave my car here till it was finished and return on the train, or the early morning bus. Now please don't worry any more."

"Oh, no. I won't worry. I'm only a stranger you picked up and I don't have to do a thing more for you of course. So now, lady, how about our running around to look over that tea room, just in case? I don't know about you, but I'm hungry as the dickens, and I don't see that eating a little snack together would injure the reputation of a schoolteacher in Carrollton, even if we are 'practically strangers.' What do you say? We've got time enough before that train gets in. But of course if you're not hungry you could sit in my car while I go in and eat. I picked up a magazine and an evening paper when I was at the drugstore. I wouldn't mind if you read them, just in case you aren't hungry."

There was a kind of a hurt grin on his pleasant mouth, and she gave him an understanding smile.

"But I *am* hungry," she said eagerly. "I'm simply starving! Let's go!" She climbed into his car again, and they drove away together.

"Now, look here," said Pilgrim as they swung around the first corner, "there's just one condition I'd like to make. Please don't let's have any more plaudits for that little act of picking you up and swinging you over my head—!"

"*Little* act!" sniffed Laurel. "Over the heads of those angry frightened cattle, you mean," said the girl. "I don't think I can ever thank you enough—"

"But listen! I'm fed up on that. I don't want to hear any more about it. Any decent man would have done the same thing, and not expected to be made a hero forever after, so please don't! If you honestly want to thank me just be a little kind and friendly to a poor soldier home on leave for a few hours, with no one to go and see. Let's eat dinner together as if we always had been friends, and were just having a nice time together. Could you do that? I won't ever take advantage of it. Honest I won't!"

She turned and looked squarely at him.

"Of *course* you won't," she said. "Don't you know I trust you? And yes, of course, I'll be delighted to have dinner with you. Then we can really get acquainted. It will be much less awkward that way. 'Old-school-friends' stuff, you know." She gave him a dazzling smile and settled back comfortably in the rattly old jalopy.

He looked at her wistfully. How game she was! How great if she really were his friend, not just playacting for the time being. But anyhow he had better make the most of it. He wouldn't have so very *many* pleasant times to remember when he was on his way to war.

"Thanks a lot," he said with a deep undertone of feeling. "That's swell of you! Well, here's the tea room. Neat little place, isn't it?"

"Why, yes, it's very attractive. I think we're going to have a nice time, don't you? It's going to be fun, soldier-boy!"

He looked down admiringly at her. She seemed almost like a little girl, out on a real picnic, and something in his warm gaze stirred her heart deeply and brought a rich color into her cheeks. It made him think of the dash of crimson on the mountain.

He helped her out of the car and together they walked up to the door.

"It's all like a picture here," she said with a little graceful caressing motion of her arm toward the flower borders of the walk, brilliant scarlet and golden autumn flowers, dashing flames of salvia, massed sharply, backed by gorgeous marigolds of all shades, deep maroon velvet dahlias, tawny groups of chrysanthemums, merging into pools of creamy white ones. "Isn't it lovely?"

They lingered together looking at them, like any other young man and maiden on their way to take dinner, and for the moment both forgot that they were strangers but a brief space before.

Inside the tables were inviting, with a few autumn roses on each, bright pretty china, and spotless linen. Phil Pilgrim seated her as courteously as any of her other young men friends would have done. It seemed all most amazing when she thought of it, only Laurel was enjoying herself too much to think of it. She had a sense of well being and she didn't want to spoil it by any questions of formality. There certainly was nothing wrong in what she was doing. She did know who he was, she had seen him as a child. That he had been working hard then in common denim overalls troubled her not at all. She had plenty of friends whose brothers were taking any positions, or "jobs," as they preferred to call them, that they could get, and glad enough to get them. Why should she distinguish between them because this young man's relatives had been poor, and he had had to work hard from early childhood? Certainly he was to be honored that he had come so far with so little help.

A waitress was by their side at once naming a long list of interesting appetizers.

"Oyster soup, oh, that sounds good!" said Laurel. "Yes, I'll take oyster soup!"

And when it came, there was no oyster in sight, but a smooth broth of rich warm tempting smell and taste, with crisp crackers of odd shapes.

An attractive tray of exotic salads of quaint fashioning and colors.

Raspberry aspic jelly, on a pale lettuce leaf with a dab of whipped cream. Orange fritters, crisp and brown with delicious orange sauce.

"But you know this is quite an extraordinary menu for a little country town," said Laurel suddenly with an amazed glance toward her companion. "Is this on the regular highway? Does it attract tourists?"

"It sure does," said Pilgrim, deciding on stuffed roast lamb for the meat course. "I never came here before, but it isn't hard to take, is it? Or to look at either."

"I should say not," said Laurel. "My, I'm glad I came here. And in such delightful company too! A real soldier. I am honored."

Their warm looks met and lingered, and a pleasant joy throbbed across the table.

"We're having fun!" twinkled Laurel with another little-girl smile.

And the light from a lost childhood he had never had answered from the young man's eyes.

When the meal was concluded, they recalled pleasant memories of a high school both had shared, till the long yellow afternoon sunshine warned them that the evening was on its way. Phil Pilgrim sat back in his chair and grew grave.

"Now," said he, "what are we going to do next? In half an hour it will be time for that train to arrive at the station, and then we shall know whether you can have your car in the morning or not. Are we ready to spring into action as soon as we have that knowledge or are there things we ought to be doing? Suppose you go and interview that woman at the desk about a possible room for yourself in case you decide to stay. And then on the way back to the garage I've thought of a couple of alternatives we might consider."

So Laurel went to the desk and Phil stood by the door looking out, a gravely pleasant expression in his eyes. He was well aware that there were days coming when he would have to pay for these few hours of unexpected happiness by deadly loneliness. Loneliness that would perhaps wear into his heart and life forever. Yet he was glad to have had this day in spite of all possibilities.

ADRIAN Faber was good-looking and wealthy. He had a fortune in his own right, and not too many relatives to meddle with his affairs. He was brilliant and accomplished, and owned a town house, a country house, a great wide log mansion up in the woods where he could house the whole hunting club on occasion, a yacht, a seashore cottage, sometimes called a "mansion," and a car that was the envy of all his friends. He was young enough to be most interesting, gay and full of delightful plans for having a good time.

On that particular Friday evening he had planned an elaborate party, to be held up in the woods at his hunt club, fifty miles away from the city, and in the opposite direction from Carollton where Laurel with a stalled car was waiting. Laurel knew these bare facts, but she did not know as yet that Adrian had been planning to make her the guest of honor, and that if his plans for driving her up to the hunt club worked out, there might be an announcement to make during the evening.

Therefore Adrian Faber was much put out at Laurel's message.

Of course Laurel had not been aware that she was to be driving up to the party alone with Adrian. She had supposed there would be a crowd, and therefore just one guest would not be missed. Anyway he had plenty of time now to supply her place with a substitute before they started.

But Adrian Faber set his handsome mouth haughtily. He didn't at all like it that Laurel had let him down and spoiled his plans. Of course there was always Genevieve but he was about fed up on her. Though—if there was no one else. It was true she might have other plans, but he was reasonably sure she would cancel anything to go to the hunt club with him. She adored the hunt club, and he really hadn't been seeing much of her lately.

There was another young man, Royal Turner, who would be at that party that Laurel was missing. He was good-looking too, in a merry kind of a way; reckless, black eyes and a little sharp black mustache. Laurel didn't admire the mustache, but probably she could persuade him to give it up if she wanted to. He had been very attentive, and had taken her places whenever she would go, plays and dances and wild rides. He was a reckless driver, and Laurel was sometimes a little afraid when she went with him. And he was always insisting that she should have a drink. Laurel didn't drink. She had been brought up with an aversion to it. Her father and mother had been against it, and they had inculcated strong reasons into her mind, why it was never the right thing to do. Laurel knew and realized dangers in drink that other young people seemed to ignore. And if she had not been taught these things, she had seen enough of the effect that drinking had on the young people she met in the gay crowd to make her hate it. Not even Adrian, with his quiet reasonable persuasiveness that a little temperate drinking was necessary in company in order to be polite, had been able to move her to yield.

Sometimes she felt that none of these young people were her natural mates, and it was in a reaction from all her social life that she had suddenly driven away to Carrollton to see about the school vacancy she had heard of through an old Carrollton schoolmate who was teaching in the city.

There were half a dozen other young men who had been attentive to Laurel while she had been staying with her cousins in the city, trying to think her way through and plan a future for herself. They were not all of this high class wealthy type. There were a couple of young writers, newspaper men, really bright and interesting, Tom Rainey and Bruce Winter. Tom had recently returned from abroad where he had been special correspondent in the war zone, and he had a mysterious air that was most intriguing. He had dark hair and a way of seeming awfully important, while yet quite casual. Laurel was never sure whether she liked him a lot, or whether she felt he was not quite sincere. Bruce Winter on the other hand had red hair, keen gray eyes, an almost rugged face, a mouth that when it was set in a firm thin line under eyes that took on a stormy look, seemed inexorable. These two men were always in the same company, though not particularly friendly. Sometimes Laurel had an idea that one of them was shadowing the other, although she couldn't be sure which was the shadowed. But they were both friends of hers, and both seemed to enjoy her company. They would likely be at that party this evening, and Tom at least would be drinking a great many cocktails. It seemed such a pity, for in many ways he was very attractive.

Then there was a young theological student who had often come to her cousin's house. He had several times asked her to go with him to hear some fine music. Chatham Brower was his name. He was brilliant, but she wasn't at all convinced that he was a Christian in spite of his ministerial intentions. She had a fancy that his recent interest in things theological might have been to escape the draft. But of course that was an unworthy thought. She had no real reason to doubt him. And he was good company. He had invited her to attend a lecture that evening, but she had declined on account of this previous engagement. He wasn't so good-looking, but he was supposed to be intellectual, and he had told her she was a good conversationalist.

Laurel, as she stood at the desk waiting for the attention of the proprietress of the tea room, remembered all these possibilities for the evening, and wondered at herself for being so content to have them wiped out of the picture, and to be stalled here with a comparative stranger whom she dimly remembered as a boy in the past. With the vision of all these city friends of hers in the offing she turned and glanced back to where Phil Pilgrim stood near their table with such a strong, dependable, fine, yet wistful look on his nice face. Handsome? Yes, but those other fellows were too, yet not one of them looked better to her than the young man who had that afternoon saved her life. And she acknowledged to herself that she was reluctant to cut short this new companionship of the day which might never come her way again.

Then the woman who had been telephoning hung up the receiver and turned toward her.

"Rooms? Yes, we ordinarily have rooms. But it just happens there is a wedding in town tonight and our rooms are all taken for the night. Tomorrow I think we shall have rooms. Could you wait until tomorrow?"

Laurel shook her head.

"I'm sorry. I need a room tonight. You don't know any place near by that I could get?"

"No, I'm afraid I don't," said the woman. "We hired

every room in the neighborhood to accommodate the people from the wedding."

Laurel went back to Phil.

"Nothing tonight on account of a wedding."

"Well, that's that!" said Pilgrim thoughtfully. "But I guess there'll be some other way. Come on, we'll go and see about your car."

They went out to the old jalopy, both thinking hard.

"What are your alternatives?" Laurel asked as she settled herself in the car.

"Well, in the first place let's see whether the generator has come yet. If it hasn't we might hitch your car to mine and run it down to the city. But of course we'd have to consider that I'm pretty much of a stranger to you, and you might not feel you cared to take a long ride like that with me, just coming nightfall!" He gave her a little grin.

"Nonsense!" said Laurel. "I certainly know enough *about* you to feel perfectly safe with you no matter how dark it is. But I am not going to allow you to take a long journey like that for me. Let's go and see about that train. Don't I hear it now?"

"Yes," said Pilgrim. "We'll drive over to the station and see for ourselves. You can't tell whether Mark may not forget to go over. No, there he is heading toward the station on a dead run. Yes, there! They've flung him a package. That ought to be it. We'll drive over and see."

Mark was undoing the package as they came into the garage, and he turned and grinned at them.

"They've sent the generator, all rightie!" he said, "and Ted and I are working overtime tonight. We'll have her done as quick as she can be done. Maybe tanight if we don't have too many interruptions."

"Great work, Mark!" said Pilgrim. "You can count

on me to bring you a pot of coffee and cinnamon buns if it keeps you late."

"Great idea, Phil Pilgrim. I see you ain't lost any of your big heart by gettin' eddicated. I'll vote for you every time."

But Laurel had been doing some thinking while the two were talking, and now she stepped up to the mechanic.

"Did I understand you to say there was a possibility that my car might be finished tonight?"

The man eyed her sharply.

"Yes, ma'am. I said that. I think if we can get this generator in before dark we might have her ready to travel by seven o'clock. Mind you, I ain't promising, not till I see what shape she's in when I get the generator in. But I think it might happen, if you don't mind paying my helper for overtime."

"Of course not," said Laurel. "It's important for me to get the car as soon as possible."

"Okay," said the mechanic returning to his work. "Stick around, lady, I'll do me best. Angels can't do no more."

She turned a quick glance toward Pilgrim but saw he had just vanished inside the room where the telephone was. She wondered whether he had heard what Mark had said. But when he was through with the telephone she would try a couple of old friends and see if either of them would take her in, provided her car was not done in time to use that night.

Phil Pilgrim came out of the office smiling.

"Say," he said with a happy grin, "want to do a little more scouting around for a stopping place? I had a hunch that I'd better find out for sure whether my man is coming on the midnight or later, and I find he came in on the five-ten. Started from Chicago sooner than he expected, and he's home now. I can see him if I drive to his house at once. I thought perhaps you'd like to go along and stop off somewhere on the way back to find a place for overnight. And anyway it would pass the time till you know for sure what to expect about your car."

"Why, that will be fine," she said smiling. "But you didn't hear what the mechanic said, did you? He told me if everything went all right he might get the car ready to move by seven. In which case I'm going back to the city tonight. I simply *must* if I can, for I have so much to do before I get back here for Monday. But of course I ought to find a place before dark where I can stay if the car isn't ready tonight."

The young man looked at her startled for a minute.

"Well, yes, I suppose he could get it done if he is willing to work overtime," he said. "Well, come on. I'm sure we can find you a place anyway, and it may help you out when you get back."

So they got into his old car again and went speeding down the road, through Carrollton, and out to a country place on the highway.

"Why, this is where Mr. Banfield used to live," said Laurel, as they turned into the driveway and drew up before the steps of a big old-fashioned brick house.

"Yes, that's the name, Banfield. Do you know him?"

"No," said Laurel, "but I remember he had something to do with a foundry down the road. I remember hearing his name. He was a manufacturer of some kind of machines, wasn't he?"

"That's right," said Pilgrim. "Now, do you want to go in, or would you rather sit here and wait? I won't be long."

"Oh, I'd much rather sit here. Don't hurry. I'm very comfortable."

She smiled at him, and he got out and went up the steps with a spring, and pulled the old-fashioned doorbell.

The door was presently opened by a girl who nodded as if Pilgrim was expected, and he went in.

Laurel sat there thinking the afternoon over with its strange happenings, amused at the situation, and still more amused at her own contentment with things. Why was it that she felt so much as if she had fallen in with one who seemed a part of her old life when father and mother were at hand, and home was a beloved and beautiful place where was protection and comfort and plenty of luxury? And why was it that she felt so much more at home in this man's company than she did when she was with any of the young men in the city who had paid her attention?

Ah, well did she know that if her cousins with whom she was staying temporarily should find out what she had been doing today, and how she had sent her regrets to Adrian Faber, and instead was staying in the company of a young man whose only contact with her in the past had been as a boy in a filling station where her father's car used to be serviced, they would lift up their hands in horror and reproach her most mercilessly.

"Laurel Sheridan! What have you done? You crazy girl!" she could imagine her friends and relatives saying. "To go off on a wild-goose chase after a job to teach school in a little dinky town, and ruin your chances to get the absolutely best catch of the city! Don't you know that Adrian Faber is simply rolling in wealth, and able to give you anything you want? And don't you know that he is just crazy about you?" Laurel could almost hear the tones of her cousin's voice as she would say these things, if she ever found out all about the matter.

But they never should know. Laurel had no intention of telling them, *ever!* If she got home tonight sometime she would simply explain that she had car trouble, and by the time she got back home it was too late to go to that party. Besides, she was tired and didn't feel equal to staying up practically all night, as it would likely prove to be. She would pass it off that way. And when and if she took that job in Carrollton she would just pass out of their picture as quietly and painlessly as possible, and let them say what they would after she was gone. They need never know about the young man who had saved her life and been so kind and interesting afterwards. That was her own secret, and too pleasant and sort of sacred to be flung into public gaze and rollicked around among kindly gossiping tongues till all the beauty and friendship were taken out of it.

Well, and then tonight, or at latest tomorrow morning, this nice young soldier boy out of her childhood's past, would say good-by and pass on to his camp or his war or whatever, and would not be around any more for anybody to jeer about. Then they would exert all the influence they had to make her snare and marry one of those wholly desirable young men whom they had so obviously flung at her from time to time.

Into these pleasant reflections came footsteps. Phil Pilgrim coming out the door and down the steps of the brick house, followed by older footsteps. A tall elderly man stood on the porch.

"Then you'll let me know, Pilgrim, not later than ten tomorrow morning?"

"Yes sir, I'll let you know if I can get my leave extended a few hours at least."

"Well, find out tonight if you can possibly get into contact with your captain. I should like to get those papers signed tomorrow for sure. I want to get the manager here to meet you tomorrow evening at the latest, sooner if possible. This thing must be put through at once."

"All right, sir. I'll do my best. Good night, sir!" and

Pilgrim swung into his car and started it, sweeping smoothly down the drive to the road, and out toward the town again.

"Well," he said in a voice half glad, half serious, "I've as good as sold my property. The government *is* going to build a big munitions factory for defense up there, and they are willing to pay a good price. It's a good thing, I guess."

"That's grand!" said Laurel. "I congratulate you. But the *government!* Do you mean *the government* is going to build up there on Crimson Mountain? Why, that's wonderful! Only why do they locate a plant where men are to work so far from town, and from a railroad? Does he know what he is talking about?"

"So he says. I don't know whether he knows or not, but he certainly thinks he does. It seems incredible that the government should want my little old parcel of land that I have always considered of very little account, but he says it does, and I shall soon find out. Probably tomorrow. The queer thing about it is my land seems to be the king pin in this plan to build up on old Crimson. You see my land has the water power, and of course they can't get along without water power. If I refuse to sell they will have to choose another site."

"But I don't understand," said Laurel. "I didn't see any water on the place you pointed out as we passed."

"No, you couldn't see it from the road, but it's there, up higher behind those thick trees beyond the house. A beautiful waterfall. It's not far from that picnic ground you spoke about. It's quite a fall, and then afterward the water winds about and down the mountain on the other side, where it finally flows into the river below Carrollton. But the water power is the reason for their selecting that site of course. I hadn't thought of that when I felt the land wasn't worth anything. But the government has offered me a nice price for the land."

"Well, I congratulate you! How nice to have that happen just now before you leave!"

"Yes, it's fine. But it means that I've got to call up my captain and get permission to stay over until this business is finished. If I can't get that it's all off, for they won't wait. They are in a hurry to get started."

"Oh, will you have trouble in getting permission?"

"Well, I don't know. I haven't asked any favors before. As this is a government offer it may make a difference. Of course Mr. Banfield is trying to arrange it from his end or I couldn't get anywhere with the captain. But even so, there's a lot of red tape in the army that can't be cut, you know."

"Well, now, drive to a telephone station right away and find out. Don't bother about me. I can find a boarding place later if I need it."

Pilgrim shook his head.

"No," he said, "it wouldn't be any use to telephone yet. He is away from camp this afternoon, won't be back till six o'clock. I've got time enough to find you several boarding places first."

"Oh!" said Laurel with worry in her eyes, "are you *sure?* I would so hate to think you missed this chance of selling at a good price, just on my account!"

"Oh, you don't need to worry about that. I guess there'll be a chance to sell all right. I'll call up at six, and then I've got to jog over to the city and see a man tonight. Too bad I'll have to desert you this evening. I'd much rather stay. But is there anything I could do for you in the city in case your car isn't fit for travel tonight? Of course I'd ask you to go along with me, but this old car isn't very comfortable. And besides I suspect it wouldn't be considered by your friends as quite the thing for you to take a long ride in a car like this, and in the *evening,* with a comparative stranger."

"Say, now, that isn't fair. Have I been treating you that way today?"

"No, you haven't," said Pilgrim smiling. "I'll say you've been a good sport. But then this would be a different proposition, to go to the city in this old ramshackle car. You know I never can be sure it will last for a long journey. I might have to spend half the night repairing it. I'm not sure but I may have a flat tire to deal with before long. But as long as the going is good I guess I can make it. Now, how about stopping at this house? They tell me Mrs. Price still takes a few boarders. It looks quiet and respectable."

"Oh, why yes, that looks nice. But, really, if you are going to the city on your own account I think I'll accept your invitation and go with you, provided you'll let me pay for the gas. However, it will do me no harm to run in here and see what the prospect is, in case *neither* of us has a seaworthy car."

Laurel was not long inside.

"Yes, it's a nice place," she said. "I told her I'd come Monday or perhaps tonight in case my car didn't get finished. Now, Phil Pilgrim, won't you please go and telephone your captain?"

"Yes, presently," said Pilgrim smiling. "We'll see how the car is getting on first."

So they went back to the garage.

"How you getting on, Mark?" asked Pilgrim as they drew up beside where he was working.

"Okay, Phil," said Mark with a grin. "Everything's fine and dandy. The lady can have her car in about fifteen minutes now. Anything more you want done, son? Say, it looks ta me ezif you needed a little tinkering yourself. You just all but got a flat tire and your engine's steaming. Wait till I get after her."

"Oh," said Laurel. "Isn't this wonderful! My car will be done in time for me to get home tonight!"

"Sure thing, lady, you hit the nail on the head," said the mechanic. "You take Pilgrim with you, and he can leave his car here till we doctor it up a bit. I can see at least half a dozen things needs doing to it."

"Thanks, Mark, but the lady and I each have our own business. If you don't mind I'll just take off my coat and get down and put on my own spare tire, and trust to luck for the rest."

"Not on your tintype, old man, you won't," said Mark. "I've owed you a thank-you for a long time for a lotta good deeds you done fer me, an' now I wantta get it off my conscience. Besides, I'm too patriotic to let you get down on them there new soldier trouser-knees with them fine creases in 'em. This one is on me, and I mean it, man!"

"Sorry, Mark, but I've simply got to get to the city. Excuse me a minute. I'll have to telephone. And when I get back I'll wager I can get my car in shape as soon as you finish that one."

So Pilgrim went in to the telephone for a few minutes and Laurel watched his face and gathered that he had finally reached his officer, and that the answer was satisfactory. It was pleasant to watch the glow of light in his eyes and the pleased smile as he talked, as if he and his captain were on friendly terms. Then he came out.

"It's okay," he said in a tone of satisfaction. "I'm off for two days longer to get this matter settled up. And now, how is your car? Why—but—what has become of mine? Mark, you sinner! What have you done with it?"

Then as he rounded the corner into the back of the garage, "What have you taken off those wheels for? I didn't tell you to repair my car!"

"Those wheels were out of alignment. Hadn't you noticed it, pal? Anyhow I'm fixing it. The lady says she wants you to go in her car. She claims she's afraid to ride to the city alone at night on that there lonely road." Mark winked affably at Laurel, as he turned back to put a final twist to a nut he was tightening in her car, before turning it over to her.

Laurel gave him an understanding grin, and turned toward Pilgrim.

"I can't credit that," said Pilgrim. "That girl's not afraid of anything."

"Listen," said Laurel, stepping to Pilgrim's side and speaking in a low tone, "this is probably my only chance to do a little repaying for the way you saved my life, and I want you please to be good and let me do it. *Please!* And besides, it *is* a very lonely ride some of the way to the city, and I really want your company."

Pilgrim looked into her wide blue eyes and something flashed from them to his own, and deep into his soul. His own glance softened.

"All right," he said, "if you really mean it. Only, remember I'm an utter stranger, you know."

"No," said Laurel, "you're *not* a stranger. Not since you saved my life!" And the smile she gave him sent a warm glow around his heart. Then her eyes went down in sudden embarrassment:

"You know I'm really quite unnerved with what I've been through this afternoon!" She explained quickly, in what she tried to make a matter-of-fact tone. "I really would feel quite uneasy alone. And besides, we have things to talk over."

He looked at her in a kind of grave amusement.

"Have we?" he asked. "What things?"

"Why, certainly," said Laurel crisply, avoiding his direct glance. "We—haven't—made—any plans yet."

"Plans?" said Pilgrim with a lifting of his brows.

"Why, yes, plans for meeting again, and all that. You haven't even given me your address."

"Address?" he said, almost stupidly. "Why would you want that?"

She gave him a quick almost reproachful look, and the color stole softly into her lovely cheeks.

"You certainly were not planning that we should go back and be strangers again, were you?" she asked almost haughtily.

He caught his breath, but held his lips steady.

"Wasn't that what you were expecting would happen?" he asked. "Isn't that what you want? I certainly wouldn't presume on some slight service I was able to render."

Laurel went suddenly white, and drew a quick breath, her lips trembling a little, though she was doing her best to hold them still.

"It certainly is *not!*" she flashed. "Why—why—I thought we were *friends!*" And now her little soft chin was trembling in spite of her best efforts.

Then the hard expression which had come into Pilgrim's face while he was speaking suddenly softened again, and he looked deep into her eyes as if he were searching her very soul.

"Are you *sure?*" he asked, and his voice was tense.

"I certainly am sure," she said very definitely. "How could you think I was like that?"

One more instant his eyes raked her face, and then he suddenly put his hand upon hers with a quick meaningful pressure, and his face bloomed into a brilliant smile.

"All right! Come on then," he said, and led the way to her car.

FILLED with a great joy that she did not in the least understand, Laurel followed him, hesitating only an instant at the car door.

"Will you drive?" she asked shyly.

"If you want me to," he said gravely.

"I do," said Laurel, and got into the right hand seat.

"Just a minute till I get my suitcase from my car," said Pilgrim, and hurried away. He was back in a moment more, stowed his baggage in the back of the car, and slid in behind the wheel.

"Okay, Mark," he called, "see you sometime tomorrow!" Then Pilgrim started the car, curving out of the enclosure and into the road, his capable hand firmly on the wheel. "I might return on the morning train you know, if I can get my work done."

He looked down at her with his charming smile:

"Well, we're off!" he said, and it seemed to mean so much more than just the words that her heart gave a queer little rapturous thrill. Then her conscience rose up in affright. What right had she to feel that way? To thrill at his words? Of course he was a good-looking soldier, wavy brown hair, nice eyes under long lashes, steady brows, clear-cut features, but what right did that give her to read into those simple words "We're off" a satisfaction of her own that perhaps did not find an echo in the young man's heart? Ah! That was a thought. Perhaps he had not *wanted* to come with her. Perhaps there was someone else he wanted to take, some other girl whom he had been planning to see and take to the city? Trouble suddenly clouded her eyes. A moment later she spoke, putting a restraining conscience into action.

"Wait!" she said sharply, "I've just thought. Perhaps this is interfering with something you had planned. Perhaps you didn't want to do this. I am being very selfish. You probably have other friends you would have liked to take with you. Or at least you must be fed up with my company by this time. I have been too insistent. Please go back. We can explain that we have changed our minds. And if I worried you by suggesting I didn't want to go alone, forget it. Or what will do just as well, ease your conscience by following me later on the same road, and pick up the pieces if any, then your duty will be just as thoroughly done. I really am not afraid."

She gave a gay little imitation of a laugh to end her words gracefully, but there was a small hurt catch like a sob in her voice that stirred Phil Pilgrim's heart more than it had ever been stirred by any girl in his life. Suddenly he laid his free hand over hers that lay in her lap by his side.

"Please don't say that," he said gently. "Please don't *think* that! I certainly *did* want to come with you. I wanted it more than anything, but I just didn't think I had the right."

"The *right?*" she asked, opening her eyes wide with a troubled wonder in them. "Why?"

"Well, I didn't feel that I should presume to drive you in your car. What would your father have thought of that? Though I may as well tell you that I was planning all the time to follow behind and look after you, without your suspecting, unless there was need. But remember I'm just a plain soldier boy you never really knew at all, and your father was Langdon Sheridan."

"My father!" she exclaimed. "Why should my father object? He wasn't a snob. My father was one of the most reasonable men in the world, and he would honor you for having looked after me."

"Listen," said Pilgrim, "I have always had the utmost respect for your father. I heard him make a speech once when I was very young. There was a lot of agitation in town about a question of moral rights, and a mass meeting in the town hall, and your father gave the most convincing speech I ever heard. He was my idea of what a speaker and a man should be. And it was because I felt that way about him that I didn't want to do anything that he might think presuming."

"Presuming!" said Laurel almost indignantly. "But my father would never think that. He would be proud that you had saved my life, and *glad* that you were taking me home! And—my mother would be glad too!"

It was the crowning word that Laurel could offer. Her lady-mother! He understood and was deeply stirred. The pressure of his hand was strong and tender.

"That was the nicest thing you could have said!" His hand moved softly over hers in a warm enfolding clasp. "Your mother was a *real lady!*"

"Yes," breathed Laurel softly, "she *was* a real lady, and she loved *real people!*"

After an instant's pause Pilgrim said softly:

"Thank you—for—that, too!"

Then suddenly there came a stream of traffic, two big trucks, and three cars dashing by, regardless of the two pre-occupied young people. But Pilgrim had seen them coming, and quickly slipped his hand from over Laurel's to the wheel. He was on the alert at once, guiding the car safely past them. Then they were alone again in the sweet quiet twilight of the country road, with a feeling between them that something wonderful had just happened, though neither of them had stopped to put the thought into logical order.

The sun was going down like a great fiery ball, in deep purple clouds, picked out sharply with a fluted cord of brilliant gold. It was like a gorgeous pageant, and the two were driving straight into that brightness, as though it had been called into being and lighted just for them.

"Isn't it gorgeous!" breathed Laurel, in a voice that was almost worshipful.

"It is," said Pilgrim reverently. And then added jocosely:

"And we have a front seat at the show. I'm glad I came."

"So am I," said Laurel excitedly. "And *look!* The sky above is getting ready for the next act. See that soft jade color stealing up above, and those dainty coral flecks of clouds dusting along to fall into line!"

Pilgrim, as he looked, thought he would never see a sunset again without thinking of her words. This was to him a marvelous experience which he must treasure in his heart, for its like would not be apt to come his way again.

They drove on through the rosy glow of the approaching night, thrilled with the beauty of the world about them, and being gradually shut in together by the soft colored twilight.

"There's only one word that describes it," said Phil Pilgrim, after they had been riding along quietly for some minutes, "and that is 'Glory'!"

He said it solemnly, in deep earnest. He did not seem at all like the same young man who had said a little while ago, "I've never had much to do with God."

Somehow that remark didn't seem to fit with his calling that display in the sky "Glory," for Glory belonged to God, didn't it? Of course there was a worldly glory, man-made—earthly royalty and all that—but one didn't speak of that kind of glory in such a reverent tone as Pilgrim had used.

She watched his profile silently for a moment, as he said it, and thought within herself that he looked as if he were in a church worshiping.

"Yes," she said thoughtfully, slowly, "that word 'Glory' is a wonderful word. It can mean a great deal—according to how you *say* it."

He turned and looked at her curiously.

"How did I say it?" he asked uncertainly.

"Oh," said Laurel, quite taken aback by the question, "well,—I didn't mean anything personal of course, but—but you *looked* and sounded as if you were worshipping God."

Phil Pilgrim looked at her thoughtfully, and then away into the dying sunset. Suddenly a cloud broke for just an instant, and let the last stabbing flame of the setting sun through. Its glow touched his face and gave it a lovely light. Laurel drew her breath in quickly. And then to cover her self-consciousness she plunged into a little story.

"I heard something on the radio the other day," she said quietly. "You make me think of it. I don't know who was talking, but he was telling about an engineer. He was a fine engineer, and was proud of his engine. One day the man who was telling this story went into the engine room to speak to the engineer and he saw that the room was spotlessly clean, everything scrubbed to the shining point, scoured white and fine. The engine itself had been polished till it shone like silver, and every joint and bearing oiled and in perfect order. And there in the little engine room near the window where he could see well, sat the engineer, his spectacles on his nose, reading *a Bible!* Very much astonished the man watched him a minute and then he spoke, a little curiously:

" 'Well, my friend, you've got a wonderful little place here! How beautifully you keep it. I never saw an engine kept so bright and shining, nor a room more perfectly clean and fine. It looks as if it had all just been made. You must have worked hard to keep it in such order. It must take a great deal of your time and patience to keep it looking like this. How does it come? You must be awfully interested in your engine room.'

"The man looked up over his glasses and smiled, a wide happy smile, and said pleasantly as if he were telling an intimate secret: 'Well, you see, I gotta *Glory*, an' I have ta live up to it!'

"And somehow the look in your face as you watched the sunset, Phil Pilgrim, made me think of that story."

Pilgrim was silent a moment after she finished and then he said quietly:

"Say, that's a wonderful story! I'm glad you told it to me. I'll be remembering it along with this sunset when I am away. Maybe I've got a Glory too, only I didn't know it. I'll be thinking about it a lot. It somehow reminds me of the look in my mother's face when I was a little kid. My mother believed in God and Glory. She had some of it in the shining of her eyes. But when she was gone I got all bitter inside and didn't think of it any more. I'm glad you've brought it back to me."

"Oh," said Laurel, "I'm glad! Thank you. And now, won't you tell me about your mother? That is, if you don't mind."

"Mind?" said Pilgrim. "Of course not. No one ever

asked me to tell about my mother before. No one ever cared."

He was silent for a moment, and then went on:

"Of course I don't remember an awful lot. I was only a kid when she died, but what I do remember belonged with Glory. That's why a sunset like this one always makes me think of her."

He was silent for a moment and then went on:

"Her people were well off—like yours, perhaps. They lived out west. I never saw the home where she lived. She had a good education. So did my father. They met in college. My father was working his way. He didn't have an easy time. Grandfather was sick and old and not able to help. Then the first world war came and took father. He and mother had got married just out of college. I was only a little kid when dad sailed for France, and he never came back. He was killed in action."

"Oh!" said Laurel pitifully. "Then you don't remember your father?"

"No," said Pilgrim sadly, "not very well. And it nearly killed mother. It broke her heart. I don't believe she ever got over it. I can remember how sad her eyes always were, even with the Glory in them. She worked pretty hard to keep us, for the money she had inherited had all been used up by her unscrupulous brother. Then finally dad's mother and father found it out and sent her money to come and live with them, but she died soon after we got here, and the rest of it had to be used to bury her. Grandmother died soon after that, and I had to live alone with Grandfather. So there you have my story. You see I'm rather a nobody, and my story isn't very exciting."

"But you came up a good man," said Laurel with conviction, "and a brave strong one."

"You don't know that," said Pilgrim. "You're just imagining. Just trying to be nice and polite."

"No," said Laurel, "I'm not. Of course I've heard a lot about Phil Pilgrim in college, what a scholar he was, and how he got quite a name in athletics, but those things don't count much in real life. Do you think so? It's what you stand for, the standards you have set for yourself, the plans you have made, whether you are steering for real things, or just want to have a good time and let it go at that."

"I see," said Pilgrim. "And how could you possibly tell by your brief contact with me, what my standards were?"

"Why, it's written in your face."

"Say, now, you are complimenting me. But I think you are all wrong. I knew a few fellows in college who had perfectly heavenly faces, and perfectly rotten hearts! Not that I'm under the impression that my face is saint-like, I'm merely trying to show you how little real reason you have to go on in judging me."

He was grinning now at her and the line of his white teeth flashed at her pleasantly. Yes, he was very good-looking, but that wasn't all. There was something fine and dependable below it that made her sure she had not misjudged him.

"Well," she said with an answering flash of humor in her own smile, "at least I have my woman's intuition to go on, and that tells me I have a right to depend on you!"

"You win!" he said with a twinkle, "and thanks awfully. But by that same token—that is, a man's intuition—I knew that you were worth saving when I decided to lift you above that herd of cattle. I took time to figure it all out, of course." He grinned. "But now, we haven't completed our family biographies yet. Won't you tell me about your lady-mother and your true-hearted father?"

"Oh, yes, of course," said Laurel. "I'm pleased that

you are interested. They were sweet, both of them. My mother *was* a lady. You have said it. Gentle and lovely always, never saying harsh things about people or to them, that I can remember. Everybody loved her. All the servants adored her. The people in the church loved to defer to her. They came to her to help in every activity, and she always helped. She had a lot of board meetings to attend, committee meetings and things. She was active in the hospital work, and in helping poor people, getting food and clothing for them, but she always did it so quietly we never even knew much about her work of that sort even at home. It was after she was gone that people came to me and told me about it. And at home she was so wonderful, the very heart and life of us all. She always had time to help us children in our play, and in our lessons, and we came to her with everything. She was so sympathetic and understanding. She played games with me, and helped dress my dolls, and was better than another child for company. All my early memories are so closely associated with her. And with my father too, when he was at home from business. We used to take trips together. Sometimes they were business trips for dad, but he always found time between to go about with us some when we went along with him on a trip, and so I grew up as their close companion. We went to church together, we took journeys together, and we talked over everything together. My older brother was away at college when I was growing up through high school days, and then, later, he was killed in an air crash, and I was the only child left.

"It was two years after that that mother died of pneumonia. She had never been very strong. And after that daddy was broken. His heart played out. And then when he knew his business was involved he went to work harder than ever, trying to save things. He was so worried that I might be left penniless. And he did manage to save some of the business. I am not entirely penniless, only just almost. But I didn't care about that. If only daddy could have stayed with me. He went very suddenly at the last. Perhaps it was the way he would have chosen if he had had his choice. But—it was very hard for me of course."

Laurel's voice caught with a soft little sound like a sob, and the tears were raining down her face, though Pilgrim could only see them as now and then a car passed and the headlights made them glisten like jewel-flashes on her cheeks.

"But—excuse me! I shouldn't be weeping," she said suddenly. "My father taught me to be brave. He didn't want me to grow up a sob-sister, he said," and she dashed the tears away.

"You poor little girl!" said Pilgrim, his hand going out to close over hers again with a quick warm clasp which she returned, and murmured a fluttery little "Thank you!"

"Now," she said, "that's about all. I've been staying with some distant cousins in the city since I graduated from college, but I wanted to be on my own, and so when I heard of this job at the Carrollton school I hustled after it. I ought to be very thankful I got it so easily. But more thankful that you saved my life, and gave me a good friend to take care of me until I got my bearings. I'm sorry you have to go away so soon. I have a notion you and I could be pretty good friends if you could stay around."

"Thank you," said Pilgrim with a sudden pang at his heart. "That is good of you. I only wish I could stay. But perhaps there will be furloughs or something occasionally. If you will let me see you a few minutes sometimes, I'll be grateful."

And so quite happily they began to talk of the future, and to discuss the war which was beginning to seem so real to them right in the near future.

As the distant lights of the city which was their present destination began to show ahead, and it became apparent that their drive was almost over for that night, they began to talk of the next day.

"What time do you have to go back?" asked Laurel suddenly. "That Mr. Banfield said he wanted to see you not later than ten in the morning. That would mean you must start back about eight or a little earlier, wouldn't it?"

"No, I think not. I shall go and see the lawyer first, as soon as I can get in touch with him, tonight if possible. And then either tonight or early in the morning I'll be telephoning Mr. Banfield," said Pilgrim. "And you? I suppose you will go back tomorrow night, or Sunday? What are your plans? I'd like to see you once more before I leave this part of the world if possible, perhaps at Carrollton for a few minutes. I want to be sure you have suffered no ill consequences from your excitement today."

"Oh, don't be silly," laughed Laurel, "I'm not a lily. The excitement won't hurt me in the least. But certainly I want to see you again as much as it is possible. I haven't so many real friends that I can let a new one go unnecessarily soon. Especially as you are a soldier! But it doesn't matter in the least when I go back. My packing can be quickly done, and I'll be ready to take you back to Carrollton whenever you say. Yes, *certainly*"—as he began to protest—"this is a round trip, and you can't get out of it. *I* have to get back to Carrollton as much as you do, and I'd much rather go *with* you than go alone."

"Oh, but surely you have friends you might want to take," said Pilgrim, "and I couldn't let you go sooner than you need to just for me."

"I have no other friends who have saved my life," laughed Laurel. "You have the first claim. And as for getting back, I suppose the sooner the better, if I have to establish a residence there before I begin to teach. Although that is quite immaterial to me. And now, where are you going to stay tonight?"

"Oh, I have an old college buddy I'll be staying with tonight if I can locate him. You know I went to college in this city for a couple of years, so I'm not without a little knowledge of the town, as well as a few friends. But in the morning I'll get in touch with you and tell you my plans, if you insist on being so kind as to want my company back. Of course I'd enjoy it immensely if it doesn't change your plans any. If I phone you by eleven o'clock would that be too late for your plans?"

"Oh, no. That will be quite all right for me. But what about Mr. Banfield? He wanted your answer by ten. I'll be ready to leave early if you say. If you call me even at eight o'clock you'll find me ready to start at a moment's notice."

He smiled.

"You're a good sport!" he said. "I wish I could have known you long ago."

"Here too!" said Laurel. "And now turn down Arden Road, three blocks, then turn right—"

They crept along from block to block, talking almost too eagerly to turn the right corners, and at last reached the cousin's house where Laurel was staying.

"Now," she said, her hand on the door beside her, "you take the car and go where you have to go, and in the morning I'll be seeing you,—or afternoon, or whenever. I'll be ready to go with you when you and the car return."

"Oh no," said Pilgrim. "Nothing doing. I'm putting your car in your garage, and taking the trolley over on the next block to my hideout in town. You know I know my way about here, and I don't intend to borrow any car. Where is your garage? Shall we drive in and then I'll give you the keys?"

They drove to the garage, Laurel insisting on going with him, and walked back together up the drive to the front door.

"If such a thing should happen as that I find I have to take an early train in the morning," he said as he handed her her keys, "would it be possible to telephone you tonight?"

"Of course," she said, "but you're not taking any earlier *train* than I can take you in my car, so please be good. I'll be ready *any time.*"

Then with a warm handclasp they parted. Pilgrim, with a lingering look back at the girl in the doorway, lifted his hat and walked quickly out into the moonlight, turning the next corner out of sight. Laurel stood for some minutes looking toward the distance where he had vanished, gave a deep sigh, then turned and hurried up to her room.

Like a small shadow she slipped past the wide doorway that led into the living room where an absorbing game of bridge was being played, and up to her own room. She was presently wildly busy taking down garments from the closet hooks, and folding them for packing. She meant to get her belongings into shape before morning, if it took all night.

Swiftly she worked, folding garments precisely in ordered piles on her bed, and on the chairs, arranging lingerie in other neat piles in the bureau drawers, and then stole out into the hall to the trunk room where luggage was kept, returning with a couple of suitcases and some bags that belonged to her.

And all this time she was listening for a possible phone call. Would Pilgrim find his lawyer, and be able to call her that night?

It was not until she finally turned out her light and slipped into bed, a couple of hours after the bridge party had gone home, and the house was quiet and dark, that she remembered Adrian Faber, and the party that was even now probably at its height. But there were no regrets for it in her heart. And her mind was too busy with the thoughts about tomorrow and its possibilities to dwell long on Adrian and his plans. Well, there was one thing pretty certain, she wasn't going to have any time tomorrow to call up Adrian Faber and make her peace with him for not attending his party last night. That would have to wait.

UP in the woods at the Hunt Club the dinner was ended, and the dancers were beginning the night of revelry.

Over in the far corner of the great ball room, two young men were standing. They had just come, not having been able to start in time for the dinner.

"I don't see Laurel anywhere, do you, Rainey? Have she and Faber had a falling out, or what?"

"*What,* I guess, is the answer, Winter. I've looked the ground over pretty thoroughly and haven't seen a hint of her. And look at Faber, devoting himself to Genevieve. He hasn't been seen with *her* for ages. I wonder what's the idea? If he's on the outs with Laurel there might be a chance for a few other poor devils like ourselves."

"Oh yes, try and do it," said the other, letting his keen gray eyes rove restlessly about the room again. "It can't be she's coming out later, do you think?"

"Don't ask me. I guess she and Faber would be the only ones who could answer that question. But say, I wouldn't have wasted my time coming up here if I hadn't thought she was coming. I've got work to do."

"What work?" asked Winter, bringing amused eyes to bear for an instant on the other's face. "You haven't got orders have you, yet?"

"Well, not exactly orders, but I've been told to be ready, and that means checking over equipment. Got to establish contact as soon as we get there, you know. Has your appointment come through yet? I'd hate to think anything would go wrong with our plans, we've talked them over so thoroughly."

"Yes," said Winter. "Say, Rainey, any idea what place we're headed for?"

"A little," said the other, lifting shifty eyes and glancing nervously around to make sure no one was near enough to listen. "Yes, a little," he added in a lower voice, "and I don't like the layout. I tell you I *don't*. Little dinky town called Carrollton, this state. Know where that is? Neither do I. And it isn't even in the town. It's up in the wilds somewhere, called Crimson Mountain! Gosh, I wish they'd put somebody with some sense at the head of this outfit. A fat chance we'll have to play any sharp detail work in a place like that, in a town in the back woods somewhere. When we get really started how often can we get off to come up to town and see any life?"

"That isn't what we joined this expedition for, is it? Seeing life?" said Winter coldly. "I guess our job is to attend to business, and trust to luck for any good times that come along. Who did you find out the location from? Dexter? Did he say it was certain?"

"No, not exactly certain, dependent on some back country lad who owns the land they want. But it seemed fairly likely it would go through all right."

"Yes? Well, what's the idea? Airplanes, or gunpowder or steel? Funny place to select for making anything like that. Did Dexter say?"

"Well, I guess a little bit of all three perhaps. Dynamite anyway. Isolated spot you know. Safe from intruders and all that. But I gathered also that there is to be some secret invention made there that is important to the country, and the outside world won't be allowed in on."

"Yeah?" The gray eyes made a flashing search of the other man's face, and circled the room again.

"Sounds good to me. But when is all this coming off? If the ground isn't bought yet they won't want us for some while, will they?"

"Oh, yes," said Rainey. "He said it was important for us to be on hand at the start, old hands, you know, in the engineering business. If they give you charge of some department they want you to be watching for fifth columnists right at the beginning. That will allay suspicion, you know."

"Look out, Rainey, that girl overheard you then, and gave you a quick look."

"Oh, girls don't count. They're too dumb to get on to a thing like this."

"I'm not so sure. Take Laurel now. She's keen as they make 'em. If she were to overhear the word suspicion used, as you did just now, she'd turn it over in her mind and maybe ask someone what it could have meant. It seems to me you ought to have been long enough in the old country, being put through your paces, to have learned that, even if you were only writing a censored column for the papers every day."

"Oh, yes, over *there!*" sneered Rainey. "One had to be careful. But this is America and nobody thinks of such a thing as finding any disloyal ones over here."

"Don't you fool yourself," said Winter. "Americans aren't dumb, and if I don't miss my guess they're waking up fast, more and more every day."

"Well, perhaps. But I think we're fairly safe from

intruders into the project, for another two or three years yet, if it lasts that long."

Winter gave him a withering glance.

"If that's your idea I don't think you'll be much use in this outfit," he said. "You'll have to get used to suspecting everybody until they are proved safe."

"What's your idea, Winter? Got a grouch on? Who do you suspect? Nobody around here, surely? I wasn't expecting to begin operations in a gathering like this."

"No?" said the man with the gray eyes. "Well, you'll have to unlearn that idea, too. Who, for instance, do you figure that colorless, stolid-looking guy over in the far corner is, and what's he here for?"

"Who? That dumb cluck over there in the dark corner looks like the devil in the deep sea watching for a submarine? I'm sure I wouldn't know. Certainly doesn't look important."

"Would you expect him to? Do you think they'd send a man that had it advertised all over him what he was?"

Rainey gave him a quick startled look.

"Meaning what?" he said. "You don't think for a minute that there'd be any of those fellows here at a gathering like this? Why Faber isn't the kind of man to invite important foreign spies to his parties."

"Oh, think not?" said Winter. "You said he advised that we come on this expedition, didn't you?"

"Yes, sure. He just wanted to give us a little change, we've been hanging around so long doing nothing. Wanted us to get acquainted and have a good time."

"Think so? Well, I don't! Not when it's Dexter who ordered it in the first place. You can be pretty sure he had a reason for sending us, and you can be pretty darned sure you'll meet up with some keen questioning the next time you see him, too. He sent us here for some reason, that's certain, and it wasn't for any nice little philanthropic idea of showing us a good time, either.

Dexter knows Faber and likely had some inside information about the personnel of this outfit, or else he planted somebody here with a special view to our presence. I think perhaps it's up to us to find out. He may be putting us to a test, you know."

"Test?" said Rainey. "Oh, you're dreaming, man. I talked to Dexter and I'm sure there wasn't any such thing in mind. He just said very carelessly that he had wangled us an invite because he thought we would enjoy it before we got into service."

"Oh, yes?" said the man with gray eyes. "Well, think again, brother. Our service began the minute we enlisted, and it's up to us to make every minute tell. I'm sure we're here for a purpose tonight, and I wouldn't be surprised if that fellow over there is the reason."

"You're crazy, Winter," protested the other man, but he lifted his eyes more than once again to look across at the stolid young Austrian with the square features and the look of withdrawal in his face.

"Think it would be a good idea if I should go over and get acquainted with him? Find out what outfit he's working with, or if he is only a dilettante?"

"Keep your shirt on, man. Don't do anything so obvious. You aren't a policeman with a badge. You won't be much good if you go at things that way. When did Dexter say he'd be likely to know positively about when we'll be moving."

"He didn't say," said Rainey half sulkily. "And it's my private opinion that it will be a long time before he knows. We're just stuck here waiting. We might as well quit and get into something else. He doesn't know what he's about."

"Hi! Rainey! It's no good to talk that way. Besides we're under orders and you *can't* quit you know. I think I'll go and have a talk with Dexter in the morning and see if I can't get some more intelligent answers than you got."

"Say! What's eating you? I didn't suppose it was so important to try and find out something he didn't want to tell. Anyhow I should worry. I can always use my time in the city. And as for swell parties like this one, you don't get so many of these in a little dinky back country town. And I'm tired sitting here waiting for Laurel to turn up. Anyway, if she did, Faber would monopolize her in spite of all Genevieve could do. You know that. We've tried it before. I'm going to get a drink. Coming?"

"No!" said Winter. "I'm going to see if I can find out why we were sent here tonight. I take it that's our first job."

"Not me!" said Rainey. "If Dexter wants my services he'll have to state what he wants of me in plain language. So long! I'm going to get a drink, and find a girl to dance with. Sit here and sulk if you want to, but I'm for a good time tonight, whatever comes tomorrow. You've got a super-conscience, and that's about as bad as having none. If you go on this way you won't last half through the war, even if it's short, and I'm not kidding!"

Tom Rainey sauntered over and got a drink, and when he looked again to the corner where he had been sitting with Winter there wasn't a sign of him anywhere. But later when he was dancing with a girl in blue and silver he caught a glimpse of Winter just going out the door with a strange young man. It couldn't be the stolid-looking one who had sat in the opposite corner alone. This one was taller. What was it about him though that reminded of the sulky stranger in the corner? Well, let Winter fool away his time trying to find a mystery at this party. He was going to have a good time, and he made a gay reply to the girl he held in his arms, and tried to forget that there was war ahead, and he was supposed to give his attention to weeding out spies. Or was he? For two cents he felt he might be willing to turn spy himself. It would be more exciting than hanging around waiting for things to happen in an orderly and military manner. Then he helped to place a gorgeous fur garment about Anice's shoulders, and together they wandered out into the clear cold moonlight.

It was not until an hour later, when they were coming back from their walk to the moonlit lake that Tom thought he saw Winter again, walking up the hill side by side with the stranger, and entering the door of the great log club house, the firelight dancing out and meeting the moonlight like clashing cymbals. Then the door closed quickly and it was gone, and the soft moonlight washed away its memory.

But when he and Anice went into the big warm room where there was still plenty of gaiety, and drinking and dancing, and many guests sitting about talking with that intimate freedom that comes at the end of an extended night of festivity, Tom could find no trace of either Winter, or the sulky stranger, and he wondered with a passing thought what had become of them. Were they closeted somewhere comparing notes, or had they gone outside once more, or were they already gone to bed?

But when at last the company finally broke up and drifted away to their night quarters, he was surprised to find Winter in the room they shared, sound asleep, so profoundly asleep that it seemed as if it might have been going on for hours.

As he crept into the bed beside his companion he had a sense of self condemnation. Maybe he should have stayed by and helped search out a reason for being here.

But in the morning when Rainey awoke his mind

immediately went to the thought that had troubled him before he slept.

"Well, how d'ya make out last night?" he asked nonchalantly, yawning slowly.

"Make out?" asked Winter fastening the last button of his vest. "How do you mean?"

"Did you find any mysterious reason for our presence in this place?"

Winter hesitated for an instant, adjusting his tie, and then answered quietly:

"Yes, I think I did."

"You *did!"* exclaimed Rainey, snapping the yawn to a brisk close. "What did you find? Was it the chump we were looking at?"

The silence this time was even longer, and then Winter answered even more quietly:

"I think I'll let you find that out for yourself, Rainey. After all when it comes right down to fundamental facts it has to be each man for himself."

"Now, Reds, that doesn't sound like you! Did you really think you had found something?"

"That's right."

"And you aren't going to put me wise?"

"No," said Winter. "I don't see that that is my business. It's something you should see for yourself if it is going to do you any good. Good-by. I'm getting back to the city. See you later!" and he walked out of the room and down the stairs. Rainey stared after him for minute and then he suddenly sprang up and began dressing hurriedly. What did Winter mean? Had he missed out on something? Was this going to hurt his reputation with the boss? Would Dexter find out that he had simply given himself to the pleasure of the moment? But no, surely Winter wasn't like that. He wouldn't give him away. And maybe, too, it was all a big bluff. Winter thought he knew it all.

He made a hasty toilet and plunged downstairs, but when he got there there wasn't a sign of Bruce Winter, and nobody knew where he had gone.

In due time certain groups of guests assembled at a late breakfast and discussed the matter of returning to the city, but Winter was not one of them, and neither could he anywhere discover the stolid-looking man who had sat in the shadows of the opposite corner last night.

Uneasily Tom Rainey hurried through his breakfast and excused himself, hurrying up to his room to look for signs of his erstwhile roommate. But there were none.

Winter and he had both brought along suitcases, and had worn overcoats, but only his own coat and suitcase remained. Winter's were gone.

He tossed his things into his case, and went down hurriedly, meeting Faber at the foot of the stairs.

"Mr. Faber, have you seen Winter?" he asked. "I seem to have missed him somehow."

"Why, no, I haven't seen him this morning," said Faber, "but he told me last night, or rather this morning, before he retired, that he was leaving early, driving down in his own car. I believe he took a couple of my guests with him who had early engagements. Mr. Schmidt and Mr. Gratz. He said he thought you would find plenty to stake you to a ride in case you decided not to get up quite so early. I believe Mr. Byrger agreed to look after you. Isn't that so, Byrger?"

"Yes," said a tall, stolid, blond man with a countenance that was so unreadable at first sight that instinctively Rainey felt indisposed to go with him. "I was just about to ask where Mr. Rainey was. I'm in somewhat of a hurry."

"Oh, thank you," said Tom Rainey stepping forward. "Greatly obliged, I'm sure, if you don't mind. I'm all ready," and he caught up his suitcase, made hasty adieus and followed the stranger, wondering what in the world this all meant, and why Winter had deserted him without explanation.

The stranger was close-mouthed and during the long ride said very little, enabling Tom Rainey to reflect on some of the quiet caustic sentences that Winter had let fall while they were sitting watching the "chump" in the opposite corner of the room last night, also the cryptic responses to his questions that morning when he first awoke. Could it be that Winter was trying to teach him a lesson? Or to give him a hint that there were enemies in the camp? Why was it that Bruce Winter could always manage to make one feel so ignorant, and that he knew it all? Well, he would show him that he could be as cautious as the next one when work really began. But why should he go around spoiling all the fun beforehand?

It was about that time that his silent companion turned to him with evident purpose and looked him over carefully.

"You were over in the old country with Winter?" he queried, scanning his features as if obtaining a photographic impression.

Rainey narrowed his eyelids and put on indifference. So! The man was going to own he was a German or something near to that, was he? Well, he wouldn't get much out of him.

"Wint tell you that?" he asked lifting his eyebrows and scanning the other's face amusedly.

"Yes, he mentioned it just before he left this morning."

"It must be so then," said Rainey. "I have great respect for Wint's devotion to the truth. You knew him over there, I suppose?"

"No, I never met him until this morning."

"By the way, I don't remember seeing you at the dinner and dance last night?" Rainey's air was of one who had felt very much at home on this expedition.

Byrger answered in a colorless voice.

"No. I didn't get here until late. Wouldn't have been here now if I hadn't come on an urgent errand."

And then Byrger lapsed into another extended silence.

Rainey, sitting there thinking, with the sound of the other man's colorless tones still echoing in his ears, tried to figure out whether in this man's smooth, brief words there had been a distinct German accent, or whether there was another nationality blended with it. Byrger! That wasn't a German name was it? Or Austrian? He couldn't be sure. During his stay abroad he had grown fairly familiar with different accents, and considered himself able to detect and recognize the origin of each speech he heard. Yet this man's speech puzzled him. Certainly he had been much in the United States, for he spoke like an American born.

And yet, why should it matter so much? Was he being put on the spot to test him?

Suddenly Byrger spoke again, watching him keenly the while.

"Have you been to Crimson Mountain?"

The question was so abrupt, so unexpected, that he barely controlled his features, barely restrained a start. So! Was this man one of their company? Or perhaps one whom they were supposed to search out and guard against? In any case Rainey was a good actor and he assumed a highly creditable drawl:

"Crimson Mountain," he repeated meditatively. "Is that some place I should have been? Certainly is a colorful name! Sounds interesting. Any reason why I should have been there?"

The other watched him speculatively, then with a slight shrug, "Could be," he said.

As they drew nearer to the city it was Rainey who spoke:

"You are in defense work?"

The other bowed gravely.

"In a way," he said. "I'm an inventor by trade."

"Yes?" said Rainey with an air of grave comment. "I should suppose that is a wide field just now in which to work."

The other made no reply, and for sometime there was silence. Then Byrger asked:

"What line are you in?"

"Oh, I'm a writer by trade," said Rainey, indifferently. "Plenty to write about in these days of course."

Byrger bowed.

"Plenty."

That was the end of the conversation until they entered the city. Then Rainey asked to be let out in front of a large printing establishment where a number of magazines and newspapers were published, and quite at a distance from the room where he and Winter made their home.

"Thanks so much for the lift," he said to Byrger. "It's been so pleasant. Perhaps we shall soon meet again."

"Well—yes," said the other. And then with an unexpected gleam in his fishy eyes he added: "Could be!"

As Rainey climbed the stairs to the office of a magazine on the fourth floor where he had at different times sold some of his articles and stories, he reflected how little he had been able to learn of his companion on that ride. Just cryptic phrases, uncanny questions, knowing looks, inscrutable silences, and a sense that the man had not only been studying him, analyzing his very soul, and accurately reading him, but also that he had been belittling him, and despising him. This was no very good report to make to Winter when he should have to account for himself to his colleague. There was nothing for it but to be mysterious, as indeed Winter had been with him the night before. He would not have to tell all he had discovered about the man, nor indeed to let it be known how very little he was really wiser for that drive to the city.

So after a brief call on his editor friend, and a briefer discussion of the article he was to write for the paper in the near future, Rainey betook himself to his room in search of Winter. And not finding him, went on to find Dexter and see if there were further orders in the offing.

LAUREL was down early that morning. She had been too excited to do much sleeping after her extensive packing was done, and she was ready to step out at a moment's notice from the cousin's home where she had been visiting.

She knew that her cousin would not be down early after her late bridge party, and it might just happen that it would be so late that she would have to be on her way, before Carolyn awoke, for she still was holding to her purpose of going whenever Pilgrim should call her. So she slipped out to the kitchen and coaxed the servant who was getting breakfast to let her have some toast and coffee at once, saying she didn't know but she might have to go away in a very few minutes in case she got a phone call.

It was while she was finishing the hasty breakfast that the telephone rang, and then she heard Pilgrim's voice: "Is that you, Laurel?" Strangely, gaily her heart throbbed with happiness.

"Yes, Phil!" and there was a pleasant eager friendliness

in her voice that did things to Phil's heart, in spite of his best resolves.

"Well, listen," he said. "I found my lawyer. He's willing to go over to Carrollton this afternoon and fix things up. I phoned Banfield and he understands it all and will have his man on hand when I get there."

"Good!" said Laurel. "That's the way you wanted it, isn't it?"

"Yes. It's the best way, of course. But see, I've got to either be there before my lawyer arrives on the afternoon train, and meet him and take him to Banfield's house, or else I've got to stay here till the noon train and ride over with him. He's going to look up all the papers, and get everything in shape and he wants to ask me a few more questions after he gets hold of my grandfather's will and the deed of the property which is in the bank. So I guess that lets you out of a heavy burden you put upon yourself, and relieves you of my company. I shall be the loser of course, but I fancy that will greatly simplify the situation as far as you are concerned."

"No," said Laurel firmly, "it won't simplify the situation at all. There are a lot of questions I have thought up during the night I want to ask you. I *mean* it, *really!* And why can't we take that lawyer over with us? Then he can come back on the train, can't he? I'm quite all ready to leave within a half hour."

"Well, that's great of you of course, but I'm ashamed to put a strange lawyer upon you."

"That's silly. I'll be glad to take him too. There is plenty of room in my car. I'm having my baggage put in the trunk at the back right now, and I'll meet you down town wherever will be convenient for you, whenever you say."

"All right, partner. Suppose I call the lawyer, and let

you know in half an hour what his reaction is. Will that be all right?"

"Quite all right," said Laurel with a lilt in her voice. Of course it wasn't going to be quite as pleasant with a strange lawyer along, but she wouldn't let a little thing like that spoil her pleasant day.

So she called the house man and got him to carry her baggage down and put it in the trunk of her car, and she carried out her wraps and some small articles to stow in the pockets of the car. Then, just as she came into the house, the telephone rang again.

"Yes?" she answered eagerly.

"Well, it's all right, Laurel. The lawyer can't go until the noon train on account of an appointment with a man from Chicago this morning, but he'll come over on the noon train by himself. He wants me to go on this morning and get some papers from the Carrollton bank before it closes at noon, and have everything ready for him so he can get done and catch the four-thirty back to the city. So, if you really are ready to start soon suppose you meet me down in front of the new post office at nine. That will give me time to do an errand, and get everything in shape, and we'll have plenty of time to talk on the way back. Okay?"

"Okay!" said Laurel, "I'll be there."

She hung up the receiver, and turning saw her cousin coming into the dining room in a becoming negligee, and smiled good morning.

"Oh, Laurel, my dear! So glad you're back," said the cousin. "I'm having some friends to dinner tonight and I needed you so much. I didn't know what I was going to do without you."

"But I'm not back, Cousin Carolyn. I just ran in to get a few things I needed, and then I'm going on. I was about to write you a little note and say good-by. I'm going back to Carrollton, and I'm not sure just how long I shall be gone. It depends upon circumstances, but I shall stay for the week-end, anyway, and perhaps longer. I'll let you know."

"Carrollton! Why, Laurel, that's absurd! That little old dinky town! You'll be missing so many worthwhile affairs. Did you have a lovely time at Adrian's party last night? I was so sorry not to have been back to see you start off. I think it's just ideal that Adrian is so attentive. I couldn't have asked anything better for you. He is a darling! And that annual party of his at his hunt club is quite famous. I felt that your fortune was simply made when you got a bid to that. Wasn't it marvelous?"

"Why, I didn't go to the party, Carolyn. I had trouble with my car and couldn't get it mended till it was too late."

"You didn't *go!* Why, how perfectly *dread*ful! How dis*as*trous! Yes, that's the right word, Laurel, *disastrous!* That party has been the talk of the social world ever since Adrian grew up. It's always in the society column, and your name was listed among the guests. Why, how perfectly *awful!* Couldn't you come home on the train or a bus? And why on earth did you go away off on a day like that when you were invited to such an important party?"

"Oh, I didn't know it was especially important, Carolyn. I really didn't think much about it. I called up of course and explained to him."

"But wasn't he furious?"

"Why, he said he was sorry of course. And I said I was sorry I couldn't get there."

"But didn't he offer to send someone after you?"

"Oh, yes, but I couldn't let him go to all that trouble. In fact I wasn't sure I wanted to go, anyway."

"You weren't sure you *wanted* to go! When Adrian

Faber is the most eligible young man in the city, and you've got him really *in*terested! You must be *crazy!* I declare you certainly are ungrateful. Here I offer you a home and all its advantages, and introduce you to the best people, and you treat the cream of the lot that way! Run off where you couldn't get back in time for the most interesting social event of the season. I'm sure I don't see why I should put myself out for you any longer when you act like that."

"Oh, I'm sorry, Carolyn. I didn't know you felt that way about this particular affair, or I would not have gone, of course. But you see I didn't realize that you cared so much. I know you have been most kind, and it was just because I wanted to arrange to relieve you of the burden of looking after me that I went away yesterday. I heard of a possible job, and I went to inquire about it. If I were permanently independent, earning my own living, I wouldn't have to be such a burden on you. I could come and see you for a little visit now and then, but you wouldn't feel so much responsibility about me. You've been sweet I know, and I do appreciate what you've done—"

"Now look here, Laurel, that's ridiculous! The idea of your getting a job! What would your father and mother say to that I'd like to know? And just when you're probably in a position to marry one of the richest and most eligible men we know. How utterly absurd! What was the matter? Did Adrian and you have a quarrel? Did you make him sore with your ridiculous idea that you won't drink? It's very silly for you to start in and try to make him over before you're sure of him. After you're married that's all well enough, but I'm telling you, Adrian has a mind of his own, and you *can't* make over a man of the world. Certainly not until you are sure you have a good hold on him!"

"Carolyn! *Hold* on him! What on earth can you mean? I have no desire to have a hold on Adrian Faber, and I do *not* wish to marry him!"

And suddenly as she spoke Laurel knew that it was true! She did not wish to marry Adrian Faber. The knowledge came like a light in the dark and troubled sky of her mind, and she felt a sudden freedom, a great release from ideas that had been trying to get possession of her. Just since yesterday the horizon had cleared and she could read her future and know what she wanted it to be. Certainly what she did *not* want it to contain.

But her cousin stood there and gazed at her as if she had suddenly lost her mind.

"Are you *crazy?* Don't you know he is *fabulous*ly wealthy? Don't you know that if you married him you would never need to want for *any*thing that you could not have?"

Laurel turned a bright face toward her infuriated relative.

"Except one thing, Cousin Carolyn."

"One thing. What do you mean?"

"Happiness." There was a clear conviction in Laurel's tone.

"Happiness! Why, you silly girl! Who wouldn't be happy with all the money they wanted, and a devoted husband to please your every whim."

"*I* wouldn't, Cousin Carolyn! There's something very essential that you have left out."

"And what is that?"

"Love, Cousin Carolyn."

"*Love!* You poor blind little goose! Don't you know that he loves the very ground you walk on? He simply *wor*ships you. I've watched him when he looks at you. It's as plain as the nose on your face. He loves you with all his heart!"

"Perhaps," said Laurel serenely, "but you see I don't

love *him!* And there can't be any right kind of a marriage without love on both sides!"

"Fiddlesticks!" said Cousin Carolyn, "Who taught you a fallacy like that I should like to know?"

"My mother!" said Laurel steadily, looking straight into her cousin's eyes.

"Your *mother!*" gasped Cousin Carolyn. "Why you weren't old enough to talk about such things when she died. She *couldn't* have talked that way to you when you were a mere child. And I'm dead certain she would never have meant to prejudice you against a promising marriage like this."

"Yes, she talked that way to me, Cousin Carolyn! She told me to remember that no marriage would be happy if there were not love on *both* sides. And I'm sure she would not have let wealth weigh in a matter like this. She said that money was not the greatest thing in the world."

"Oh yes? Well, that was easy enough for her to say. She always had plenty of money for any whim she chose to indulge. She never knew what it was to scrimp and save in order to get a new evening dress or a mink coat. Your father was a rich man, Laurel, and you were brought up with expensive tastes. You've got to think of that when you come to picking out the man you want to marry, and you ought to be glad enough when you find a rich one who is ready to fall at your feet."

"I'm sorry, Cousin Carolyn, but I don't agree with you, and I'm not trying to 'pick out' a man to marry. I'm not going around trying to ensnare *any*body, as you suggest, nor to get a rich husband. When the right one comes and we love each other, *if* he's a good man who has a right to marry me, that will be a different matter. But unless that happens I'll go free and unmarried and try to like it. That's the philosophy my mother taught me. And now, Cousin Carolyn, I'm terribly sorry to disappoint you after all your kindness, but I'm going away, and you won't need to worry about me any more. I'm going among some of mother's old friends, people that my father trusted, and I'll be perfectly safe."

"But you can't just visit your mother's old friends forever," said the cousin with scornful eyes. "You'll *have* to get married sometime you know. And you may never find such a fine husband as Adrian."

"No, I don't *have* to get married *ever* unless I want to," said Laurel with a lift of her chin that seemed like a challenge. "Why do you say I'll *have* to get married sometime?"

"Why, Laurel, be sensible! Who would support you? You have nothing of your own, or that is practically nothing. Who do you think would support you? Goodness knows *I* can't. John's very likely to lose his job and have to take a less lucrative one, and Grandma Howson has just enough to get along on as it is. So, of course you'll find out what you have done—probably when it's too late! But honestly, who do you think will support you if you don't get married? I've been doing everything I knew how to make a good marriage possible for you, and you act this way!"

Laurel gave her cousin a look of amused astonishment.

"For Heaven's sake, Carolyn, I'll support *myself,* of course. What did you think? I certainly never would have come here at all if I had known that you had any such idea. I only came for a little visit anyway, and it is high time I was leaving if you've got an idea you have to bring in suitable husbands for me, to get me off your hands."

"Now, Laurel, it isn't like you to be bitter and resentful," said the indignant cousin. "You've lost your head and your temper. You will regret this, Laurel, and be writing and asking me to forgive you and let you come back."

"Sorry, Carolyn, I'll ask you to forgive me now, if I've done anything that has hurt you, but honestly I don't *want* to come back. I've definitely decided that this kind of a life is not for me. Now don't let us part in anger. Kiss me good-by, dear. I've got to go now, but I'll be writing you when I get located, and let you know where I am."

Laurel put her arms softly about her cousin's neck and pressed a gentle kiss on the cold haughty cheek, and then, picking up her handbag and her little overnight bag, she hurried out the side door to the garage, got into her car and drove away, to meet Phil Pilgrim down in front of the post office.

Cousin Carolyn heard the car go down the drive, and waited an instant for it to stop in front of the door. Surely Laurel wouldn't go off permanently that way. Surely she would return and try to argue the matter out, and she of course would be able to show her definitely how impossible it was for her to run away from such great opportunities as were opening up before her. Surely she would be able to make her understand, too, how mortifying it would be to herself to have such a thing happen, after this precious prince of an Adrian had given signs that he was more than pleased with her, and was ready to let it be known that he had a special possessive right in her. Surely—

She listened, but Laurel's car went right on down the street. It did not stop! And Cousin Carolyn rushed to the front door and began waving her napkin which she had snatched from the dining table frantically.

"Laurel! Laurel!" she called, her voice rising above its usual ladylike cadence. But Laurel's car had turned the corner and she was on her way to meet Phil Pilgrim, her heart singing, for no reason she could even try to understand just then.

And in a moment or two Cousin Carolyn became aware of a pompous neighbor who had stopped in his daily promenade around the block with his daughter's two Pekingese pups, lifting his hat gracefully inquired if there was anything the matter, and where *was* Miss Laurel? Could he do anything about it? Which way did she go?

"But I don't see her car anywhere, Miss Carolyn," he said, flustered almost to confusion. "Where do you think she has gone? Would you like me to go into the house to the phone and call the police?"

And then Cousin Carolyn became aware of other neighbors looking out their front doors, and a general flutter of excitement in the street, and was suddenly aware of her permanent wave still set under its protecting net as she had arranged it when she retired last night.

"Oh, no, thank you," she managed in her most approved manner, "it's really of no consequence whatever. Just a little matter that was forgotten, but it will do when she returns."

And then Cousin Carolyn retired behind a firmly closed and locked front door, and went breakfastless to her room to reflect on what a very foolish girl had done to spoil her best laid plans to bring affluence into the family.

But Laurel was sitting in front of the new post office, watching for Phil Pilgrim.

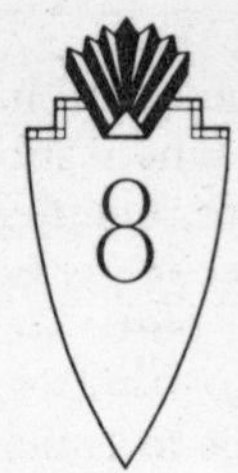

LAUREL drew up her car in a vacant space before the new post office and sat watching for the approach of Pilgrim, thinking over the twenty-four hours since she had started out toward Carrollton in search of that position as a teacher in the high school. Suppose she could be set back twenty-four hours, and knowing all that would occur, what she would go through, what she would find in the woods, on the highway, in the town, in the office of the school board, and all that she would now leave behind in the city and miss out of her life afterwards, would she have gone? She looked the question firmly in the face with the echo of Cousin Carolyn's last few paragraphs still ringing in her ears, and answered in her heart, promptly, firmly, eagerly that she would.

No, she was not sorry that she had taken the step. Uncertain as she had been when she started, she would not go back if she could, now, and have it undone. She was glad she had gone. Glad she had signed the contract and agreed to take the position in the Carrollton high school, glad she had packed her belongings and faced her cousin, and started. It might not turn out to have been the finest thing she could have done, but she had no regrets. Not even when she thought of Adrian's wealth. She did not care whether she ever saw Adrian Faber again or not, except perhaps to apologize again for having deserted the party so at the last minute. In fact she preferred not to have to, for she was morally sure that even if she got in touch with him if only by telephone he would somehow contrive to hinder her, and coax her into something, and she did not wish to be annoyed that way now. Also there was another thought. She had something pleasant to finish, the time for which would soon pass by, and might never return her way, and she simply must not let anything hinder her in it. She would not have missed knowing Phil Pilgrim for anything else the world could hold. So she waited in her seat, and kept well to the side of her car, not putting herself in a position to be readily recognized by anyone she knew who might be passing, and faced the thought.

She had never known any young man exactly like Phil Pilgrim, and she wanted to study him, to find out if he was really what he seemed. She must. She felt it was imperative, and would have a bearing on all such questions as she had just been discussing with her aristocratic cousin. And to her mind there came a memory of his sunny smile, that seemed to tangle in her heartstrings, and create a lovely song.

It was then she saw him coming, a suitcase and a brief case in his hand, walking slowly in earnest conversation with another man.

She liked his looks again as she watched him approach. She was glad he was good-looking of course, but she had a feeling as she thought about it that she would have been just as pleased to see him coming, even if he had been quite homely and lacking in manly grace. She would have known at least that he was someone whom she could trust.

And those other men with whom she had been going about more or less for the past six months, she had never felt she could quite trust. Oh, not that they would not usually tell the truth, except perhaps on occasion, but they were none of them, not even that minister, men of whose reactions to grave questions, even of right and wrong, she could always be sure, unless it was obviously to their own personal advantage. Their standards were not the ones by which she had been brought up.

Of course Cousin Carolyn would sneer at that and say those standards were outmoded, and that times had changed since her mother and father were young and had the jurisdiction over her. But she knew better. She knew that those old-fashioned standards were dependable in times of stress, in trouble and uncertainty. She had seen it tried, and she knew there would be no peace in trusting men whose standards were otherwise. As far as she knew since she had come out of college she had not seen many young men whom she could even *think might* be dependable in a time of disaster. Phil Pilgrim was the only one she felt sure had even approached to the standards she knew.

Oh, she was not searching the world over to find a trustworthy man *to marry.* She was not considering marriage now. Perhaps she never would. She was only trying to adjust her world to a set of friendships upon which she could rely. If one could not have a few young friends in whom one trusted, what was life worth? And so she wanted to study Phil Pilgrim and see if he was really what he seemed to be. There was no harm in that. He would soon be gone out of her neighborhood, and there was no danger for either herself or him in having a friendly investigating talk for a couple of hours as they went on their way together. She wanted to settle the question once and for all whether a young man in this age *could* be what he had seemed to be.

And then he stopped opposite the car, and turning looked at her an instant and gave his bright smile. That look in his eyes made her heart give a wild little plunge, just as it had done yesterday. Well, perhaps it hadn't been wise in her to come after all. One could *miss* a look like that, a smile like his, terribly, if one got too used to it. Yet, she was *glad* she had come, and she felt a restful sense of protection as he stood there for an instant talking with the man who had come with him. Then the stranger turned, lifted his hat slightly, said: "Well, I'll see you this afternoon," and went up the steps of the post office and out of sight.

Laurel slid over to the right of the driver's seat, and Pilgrim got in, shut the door, and quietly threaded his way through the rapidly increasing traffic, and out to the highway that led from the city.

"Now," he said when there was comparative quiet, "is there anything you want to do before we leave this region, any errand? Perhaps I should have asked you sooner, but there is plenty of time as far as I am concerned, to do a few small errands yet, and still reach our destination in time."

"Oh, no, thank you," she said. "I haven't any errands that I can't do later by mail or telephone, and I'm only too glad to be done packing and be on my way. You know this isn't my home town, and so I'm not breaking my heart over leaving it."

She gave him a quick bright look, and saw he was studying her earnestly.

"Then you didn't meet with any opposition from your friends and relatives about your going away so suddenly?"

"Oh, yes, a little," she laughed lightly. "They thought I was an awful fool for going to work instead of loafing around and playing through a brilliant social season. That is the reason I am glad to be gone as soon as possible lest I may meet some more of them, and that kind of opposition wears me to a frazzle. Their ideas and enjoyments are so entirely different from mine. What makes me happy would be boresome to them. We aren't constructed on the same lines. So I'm glad you arranged to start early, because I'm certain if I had lingered around a little longer there would have been a strong opposition organized, and this way they don't know where I am and can't even try to stop me until I am thoroughly established in my work."

"Have they any right to stop you?"

"No, not a particle. They are just cousins whom I have been visiting this summer. They would like to run my life for me. But I'm of age you see, have been for six months, am not in any way dependent on them. They haven't even the right of close beloved relatives, who really love me. They are fond of me in a way, if I'm a credit to them in the social life they lead, but they do not love me. They are merely *fond* of me, like to have me around. They do not really love anybody but themselves."

She spoke more as if she were arguing out the matter for her own satisfaction than to be giving information to her companion, and she ended with a pleasant little laugh.

"I see," said Pilgrim with a friendly smile. "I've known people like that. There seem to be a great many of them in the world. Well, in that case we don't have to feel sorry for them, do we?"

"Not at all," laughed Laurel. "And yet it seems rather awful in me, doesn't it, to be talking that way about people who have really been very kind to me, and done their best to have me meet the best people in their social class. I shouldn't have said all this, but I'm fresh from a pretty hot scorching conversation with my cousin, and I feel a bit indignant at her."

"Well, then, we won't include her in the conversation at present. Wouldn't that be best? May I tell you about what my lawyer advises?"

"Oh, do, please. I'm very much interested. Did he think the sale would go through all right?"

"Oh, yes. He thinks it's great that I have this opportunity to sell. But he thinks I should have a better price than even Banfield suggested. He insists that *he* will arrange that. He seems to know what the government is paying for such lands, and he thinks Banfield is planning to make a pretty penny out of it himself. I think he may find himself grandly mistaken when he meets up with Banfield, but he wants me to let him manage the sale, says he is my lawyer. And of course I'm glad to do that. He was a good friend to my grandfather, and it happens he knew my father before he went away to war."

"Oh, I'm so glad!" said Laurel, exactly as if she had been really a friend of the years, and not just an utterly new acquaintance.

A pleased light came into the young man's eyes.

"It's good of you to care," he said. "You don't know how pleasant it is to feel that there is somebody interested in my affairs. You can't be in the army for very long without feeling very much alone at times, when it comes to private affairs. And you see I haven't been there long enough to search out a few intimates yet."

"Why, certainly I'm interested," said Laurel. "You see in a way I'm much in your position. I have cut loose from the things and people I have been with of late, and I'm going into a new world, even though it happens to be in the same vicinity where I spent my childhood. Still it has changed a lot of course, and the people I knew either aren't here any more, or else I haven't found them yet. We'll just play we're two babes in the woods today, finding our way, shall we? And I certainly am glad the matter of the sale of your property is going through all right."

"Yes," said Pilgrim. "It certainly will be nice to have a little money in the bank, instead of utter nothingness, when this war game is over, if it *ever is!* It will make all the difference in the world to know I'm not absolutely penniless. Of course Grandfather hoped his land would be worth something for me, some day, but he never dreamed of anything like this kind of a situation, the government paying good money for that old isolated ground."

"But what about the two graves?" asked Laurel gently, thoughtfully. "What will become of them? I think I shall always remember those two white headstones with the soft light sifting through the crimson foliage on them. They were sweet. I think if you don't mind, some day I'd like to take some flowers up there and lay them on those graves. Of course I know the two people buried there couldn't know about it, nor care. Me a stranger to them! But maybe God would see. He might even let them know about it, how I enjoyed doing it, because you, their grandson, had helped me when I was so frightened. It's just a thought, a little gesture of gratitude, I know, but if you don't mind I'd like to do it. A kind of memorial of the day we met."

Her face was very earnest as she spoke, and she lifted her eyes to his and met the deep tenderness there that was almost like hidden tears.

"It is a lovely thought," he said, his voice deeply stirred. "It is something I never could afford to do. In fact I never thought to do it. There were not many flowers in my life, especially not in those days. I put the stones there as a mark of respect. It was the only way I had to express my sorrow, and my gratitude for what they did for me. But to answer your question about the graves. I had thought of them, and I have been hoping I can save that lot over the other side of the road from the house where they are located. At least until sometime later, when I would be able to have the graves moved to some more permanent place. But now, if this deal goes through, I can afford to have them moved at once perhaps. Maybe that would be better. But I do appreciate your thought of the flowers. It will hallow the spot for me whenever I think of it, just because you have spoken of doing it."

She looked at him and smiled understandingly, a soft pink flush in her young cheeks.

"But there is one thing I must insist on," he said after a thoughtful moment of quiet. "I want you to promise me that you will never go up to that lonely place alone, especially after this munitions plant is started. You know there might be a lot of rough characters around while building is going on, also dynamite and gunpowder. It wouldn't be safe for you then. Will you promise me that?"

She gave him a startled look.

"Oh! Do you mean *our* country is going to get like that? Not safe to go anywhere?"

"I don't know," he said sadly, "one can never tell what war may bring—if we are invaded. But around munition factories I wouldn't say it was a place for women to go, at least not in as isolated a place as that. I don't fancy you'll find cattle prancing around so promiscuously as yesterday, perhaps, but until things get going so you can be sure what you are getting into, I wouldn't like to think of your going alone even for some beautiful attention to my dead relatives."

"All right!" she said quietly, "I promise. Although I've been so accustomed to think of old Crimson as a safe place that it is hard for me to realize it could be anything else, even in war."

But she sat very still thinking for some minutes after that. Finally she asked: "About what time do you think you'll be through with your business this afternoon?"

"Oh, I don't know. I shouldn't think it would take long. Why? Is there anything I can do for you?"

"Well, I'm not sure, but I thought if you had time I'd like to get you to go with me somewhere. What time do you have to leave for camp?"

"Oh, well, I *should* be back there Sunday night, but the captain told me if the business was not completed until Monday I could have another day, so there is no special hurry. We are likely leaving our present camp in another couple of days, so there won't be so much to miss, and evidently word had got to the captain that I was needed here till the deed was fixed up, a lot of little formalities to be looked up and so on. So I'm reasonably sure I shall have time to do anything you would like done."

"That's nice," she said. "Well, I'll let you know. Want to come to my boarding place for dinner tonight?"

"You going to that last dump where I took you yesterday?"

"Well, I'm not sure. I thought of another place I might try first. I want to get the lay of the land and see if there is anything better before I settle definitely. Perhaps it would be better to meet somewhere when you get through at Mr. Banfield's and then I can tell you my plans?"

"All right. I'll do that."

"That will be fine. I'm sure I ought to be able to get things settled in my mind by that time. Now, let's talk. I'd like to know all about your college life. I'm sure we must find some mutual friends somewhere. Did you ever happen to meet Rita Bryson? Or Lorne Meredith? Or Casper Challenger? It seems to me I've heard one of them speak of you."

"Oh, yes, I knew Challenger. He was in my class when I was a sophomore. Not Meredith, though. He graduated two years ahead of me, and though I remember him I didn't get to know him well. I've heard of Rita Bryson of course. She was pretty well known, but as I didn't move much in the social circles I never came into contact with her. But say, you must have heard of Gale Carson and her brother Plumfield. Plum Carson was my roommate for awhile when I first went to College, and I sure liked him a lot. I often heard him speak of his sister, Gale. She must have been in your class, wasn't she?"

"Yes, she was."

And so they plunged into eager talk about their college days, discovering more and more mutual acquaintances, and beginning to feel very much at home with one another.

And then, all too soon, Carrollton appeared in the distance.

Pilgrim looked at his watch as they saw an inviting looking restaurant just ahead.

"How about it if we take a bite here, before we get to town?" he asked. "Then we can take things easy afterwards. Are you hungry? Or would you rather wait awhile?"

"I'm hungry as a bear," said Laurel. "I really was too excited to eat much this morning, what with listening for the phone and getting my baggage into the car before Cousin Carolyn came down stairs and discovered my plans. And then when she did come she raised such a song and dance that I couldn't have swallowed a bite more to save me. I hope you're hungry."

"I certainly am, for I didn't stop for breakfast at all. Was too busy getting things in line for my departure. I think I could eat an ox if it was well cooked."

They went smiling into the neat-looking restaurant, and life again became a delightful adventure. Another resting place where they could push aside for a little while longer the fact that they might very soon have to part forever.

"And now," said Pilgrim as they finished their meal, "we've just three or four minutes to settle a few important questions. In the first place, here's one I spent a good deal of time on last night and decided that I wouldn't leave you again without asking it and getting your answer. If during the months that are ahead I should dare to write you a letter now and then, or send you a mere postal card at times, would it offend you?"

Laurel flashed a pleasant look at him.

"It certainly would not."

"And might I hope that now and then I might receive a word or two at least in recognition?"

"You certainly might," said the girl again. "Aren't we friends and why shouldn't we write?"

Pilgrim drew a long breath.

"That's a load off my mind," he said. "Do you know I really haven't any folks of my own to write me, and I'd like it a lot if I might feel I had one sympathetic friend who sort of took a little interest in what happened to me. You know it's a lonesome time at camp when all the other fellows are getting letters and there's not even an advertisement for me. I haven't been in camp so long yet, but I've had a chance to experience that already. Oh, of course I know a lot of fellows from college and places where I've worked, but somehow fellows don't write much, and when you've not had a home for years a letter certainly would be appreciated. It sort of seemed to me as if *you* might understand, and not think me too presuming, even if I haven't known you very long."

"Of course!" said Laurel trying to keep back the brightness of forbidden tears, that would make her eyes shine in spite of her. "I'm glad you asked me. I'm not sure but I would have written to you anyway, at least once, even if you hadn't asked. One doesn't get lifted over the heads of wild cattle every day, and one doesn't forget afterward, and never think another thought about the one who did it. Of course I'm answering your letters and cards, and you are not to think I'm forward either if I should happen to write sometimes ahead of the right order. Remember you aren't the only one who is starting out on a new life and leaving the old one behind, and I'm going to be plenty lonesome myself. You see the crowds of friends I have back of me won't in the least understand why I'm doing this, deliberately leaving what they consider fine opportunities behind me and setting out to earn a plain living and just be satisfied with that. They don't understand and they won't forgive it, and therefore they won't write to me. And to tell you the truth I don't much care if they don't, most of them, just because they can't possibly be in sympathy with me. I sort of think you will understand," and she twinkled a wistful little gamin grin at him.

"Thank you," he said. "I'll do my best to be a sympathetic friend if you'll give me half a chance. And now, next, suppose you drive to the filling station at three o'clock where we left my car yesterday, and I'll telephone you there and let you know the prospect. There's a possibility of course that I may not be free to go with you until after the four-thirty leaves, if I have to put that lawyer of mine on the train, but I ought to know by three what is likely to be happening. Will that be time for what you want?"

"Oh, yes. Yes, indeed. But please don't put yourself out to go with me. It isn't really *necessary* you know, just pleasant!"

"I see," said Pilgrim smiling. "That sounds good. Somehow I feel like a regular guy, making plans this way with a girl. You know I've never had many girl friends, in fact not any real ones. Just acquaintances, or schoolmates, and only a speaking acquaintance with those."

"Well, I'm afraid you have one now," she laughed. "And, now sir, does that finish the list of questions?"

"No," said Pilgrim. "There's one more thing I wanted to bring to your notice, and that is a dear little lady who used to be a good friend of mine when I was a kid. That is she always took me into her kitchen when I delivered eggs, or fresh berries I had picked, and gave me hot gingerbread, or bread and honey, or fresh sugary doughnuts, and acted as if she had some interest in a mere kid beyond his being a delivery boy. She used to ask me if I knew God, and if I knew how to pray, and once she gave me a little leather Testament, small enough to carry in my pocket. I've kept it always, and taken great care of it, kept it wrapped in tissue paper and all that. But when I knew I was going to war I hunted it out and put it in my pocket. I sort of thought I'd like to have it with me."

Almost shamedly he reached his hand in his breast pocket and drew out the little soft leather Testament and handed it to her, opening the flyleaf on which was written in a fine old hand,

To Philip, with my love and prayers,
M. C. Gray

There was a tenderness in the eyes of both as Laurel examined and admired it, and then handed it back, and he returned it to his pocket.

"That is beautiful," said the girl earnestly. "I'm glad you brought it with you. If I were you I would read it a lot. Perhaps it will help you bear things when you are lonely."

"I'm going to," said the young man. And then after a

moment of thought, "I suppose it will be sort of an odd thing to do to read a Bible in camp among a lot of fellows. There won't be much quiet there. But there'll often be woods where I can go away by myself. Somewhere I'll find a quiet place. However, I'm glad I have it. But that's not what I meant to talk about. I just showed it to you so you would see what kind of a little woman she is, and I thought perhaps, it might be, *you* would like to know her. She would be somebody you could go to if anything troubled you, and you hadn't found the right old friends of your mother's yet. Would you like to meet her if I were to take you there and introduce you? It wouldn't take long, just a minute or two. And I must tell you first that she isn't rich nor fashionable. She lives in a little cottage, and is very plain and simple. She hasn't much money I'm afraid, and she couldn't do much for you in a worldly way, but when you said that about your friends not understanding you, I couldn't help but think of her. She's the understandingest woman outside of my mother that I ever knew. She even seemed to understand what a kid who brought her eggs was thinking about and wanting, and her smile was worth a million. Of course I don't know how things have gone with her since I went away, but Mark tells me she still lives in her little bungalow so I thought I'd tell you about her. But if you'd rather not, why it's all right with me."

"Oh, I'd love it!" said Laurel, her voice full of tears. "I do hope you'll have time to take me to her. Does she know you are here?"

"No. I haven't thought of her in years till I came on the little Testament when I was packing up things from our house. And I never felt really well enough acquainted with her to go and see her on my own account. She was just one of those folks you sort of think you'll likely meet in Heaven—if there is a Heaven—and you should happen to get there."

"Oh, there *is!*" said Laurel with sudden conviction. "I'm sure there is! And you must—we *must* get there!"

"Perhaps!" said Pilgrim with a sudden dreamy look in his eyes. Then he glanced down at his watch.

"Time's up!" he said. "I must call up Banfield and collect my car and then meet that noon train. Shall we go?"

"Yes," said Laurel rising hurriedly, "go quickly. I've allowed you to stay talking too long. So long! And I'll be waiting for your call at three at the garage. Come, we must drive there this minute!"

AFTER Laurel had left Pilgrim at the garage, and seen him drive away in his own car she drove at once to the boarding place which Pilgrim had designated as a "dump," and took the room she had seen the day before. It had seemed to her a possible abiding place, at least for a few days until she could get her bearings and look about a bit. But she did not take it permanently although the landlady tried to make her do so.

"You know there's talk we're going to have a big munitions place put up here, and if that's so—and I guess from all I hear it is—why, there'll be great call for rooms. I've had inquiries from three or four men who are heads of departments or something, and so, if you should be wanting this for all winter, you better get your bid in now. I ain't sure I could let it at this price if you wait too long."

Laurel looked the woman over as she was talking and decided to take the chance. The room was pleasant enough but what of the men? Would they be unpleasant? That was a chance one took in going to a boarding house of course. She didn't mind how rough they might be, working men probably, but there might be some who would be fresh and unpleasant. Well, it was best not to be too definite about this at the start. This wasn't the only boarding house in town of course, and she would just try it out and see.

"Sorry," she said firmly to the hostess, "my plans are not definite yet. I'll take the room for a week, until I see what I am going to do. I may be going to some friend for a time, or I may not remain in town long."

So the house boy carried her bags up to the room she had selected, and she took the key the landlady gave her, locked her door, and was presently on her way.

There were three old friends of her mother's whom she had planned to interview first and perhaps get some advice about a stopping place. But she had wanted to have an abiding place before she looked them up lest they would feel obliged to invite her to stay with them. And she didn't want to be under anyone's wing in that way. She had had enough with Cousin Carolyn, trying to find eligible young men for her, to want to run the risk of any more of it.

But when she drove about her old home, she found that the neighborhood had changed quite a little. The handsome old frame house where Mrs. Sanford, her mother's friend, had lived, was being torn down for the erection of an apartment house. There would be no refuge there. The workmen of course did not know what had become of Mrs. Sanford, but a question to a child who lived next door brought out the fact that Mrs. Sanford had gone west somewhere to live with her married son. Another one of her family's friends, Mrs. Hargrave, was reported to be in the hospital in a nearby town, seriously ill. The third friend, Mrs. Honeywell, had gone to Florida for the winter, and might not be going to return at all if she liked it in the south.

Laurel turned away from the former Honeywell door

disappointed. She had longed to see some of her mother's old friends, and to feel that she was not entirely a stranger in a strange land. But evidently it was not so planned for her.

There were other old friends, of course, but they were somewhat scattered, and none of them were people she wanted to turn to just now before she had her plans fully made. Some of them were too possessive and would be Cousin Carolyns, and others would think they had to turn Heaven and earth and take her right in, and she did not want that. Besides, she had a number of things to do. She wanted to look up the school superintendent, and talk with him a few minutes, get an idea of her job and what was expected of her.

She glanced at her watch. Time was hastening on. Three o'clock would arrive before she realized. She certainly must hurry.

There was one errand she had decided upon, so before her interview at the school she drove to a florist's shop.

Carrollton did not have a very large selection of flowers, but she remembered that in her little-girl days they always had roses, plenty of roses. And roses of course would be right. There ought to be chrysanthemums now, but somehow they did not seem just the thing she wanted. They were too big and arrogant. Roses seemed the fitting thing to lie softly below those two white stones near the roadside. Besides roses would wither quietly and not make great brown clutters over those lonely graves.

She selected the flowers carefully, lovely white buds, a mass of them. How sweet they were! Short stemmed to lie yieldingly over the pitiful mounds. Some pale blush roses, for the little sweet grandmother. Somehow she felt that there must be something of sweetness in a grandmother of Phil Pilgrim. Anyhow they would not be obtrusive, flaunting themselves to the passers by on that grim road.

Of course, it might be that Phil Pilgrim wouldn't have time to take her there, and she mustn't break her promise to him, not to go alone. In fact, since her experience with those steers she shivered at the thought of ever trying that road again alone. But if he couldn't take her there today, perhaps it might be he would find he had to wait over until tomorrow, and there might be time then. At least, she would tell the florist to arrange the flowers in the box with some wet moss about their stems. They would surely keep one day. And if there were no other opportunity to take them now, she might find someone else she knew to give them to. At least she would do her best to get them ready for whatever might come. There was a sweet look on her face as she watched the flowers being disposed in their bed of damp moss.

So, with the big box in the back of her car, Laurel started on again. She made her call on the superintendent, fortunately finding him in the office at school, and had a brief talk with him, asking a few questions she had been pondering over in the interval of the night, and decided that he was going to be pleasant to work for. She had no idea how pleasant she looked to the superintendent who had not liked her predecessor, and moreover was feeling rather forlorn in the town of Carrollton, far away from most of his friends. He did not look upon Carrollton as the ultimate place of his desires anyway. Laurel was a lovely girl and it wasn't going to be unpleasant to have her around. A nice thing to look at.

He took Laurel into the room of which she would have charge, explained the rules of the building, the hours of her day, went over the list of the scholars for that grade, and was generally helpful.

She glanced at her watch as she came down the walk to the car. It was almost time to go to the filling station for Pilgrim's call. She would drive around by her old home and get just a glimpse of it, and then go straight to the garage.

It was the first time she had seen the old home since she came away from it a few weeks after her father's death, and the casual look she allowed herself to give it as she drove slowly by now was almost too much for her. It seemed so stark and desolate and alone. Sold to strangers, who hadn't cared enough about it to keep the grounds in attractive order, or to put pleasant curtains at the windows. She did her best not to see these things as she passed, and putting on speed tried to blink back the tears that sprang to her eyes. How her longing heart had wished to see the old familiar things, how her eyes had unknowingly looked for loving faces at the windows. Oh, had she been wise to come back to Carrollton? It never could be the same of course. Would it ever grow bearable, living this way, a stone's throw or so from the home that had been so dear, always looking for the precious mother and father who had been so much to her?

She stepped on the gas and hurried forward, turning into the next street blindly, and bringing up sooner than she intended to at the garage.

She had them put gas in her car, check the oil and water, and polish up the windshield. Then, full five minutes before three she heard the telephone ring, and Mark called her to come.

She chided herself as she heard Pilgrim's voice for the pleasure it gave her. Now why should she feel that way for a person who was a mere stranger yesterday? But she did.

"I'll be there in half an hour," he said. "Will that give you time for what you want?"

"Oh, yes," she said with a glad ring to her own voice. "Are you sure you can spare the time?"

"I sure can!" came the answer, as glad as her own.

So she sat in her car by the side of the road and looked off at the hills, lovely in their autumn dress. Crimson Mountain! What a lovely name, and a gorgeous mountain! And to think it was to be used for commercial purposes! It seemed such a shame to have the wonderful trees messed up with tall chimneys puffing smoke among the brilliant foliage, screaming whistles calling men to their labors. And yet she was glad that Pilgrim had been able to sell his land, and to sell it well. Perhaps it wouldn't be such a blot on the landscape. It might be that it would be hidden from the town, and that the places she knew would not even be able to see what had come to Crimson Mountain.

And then she heard the sound of his car coming and her heart quickened. He was coming! The color sprang to her cheeks and a light to her eyes, though she had no intention of looking like the personification of joy, and wouldn't for anything have had him know how glad she was to see him.

But he saw it, and his own heart was filled with a great joy, which was quite all wrong for a soldier about to go back to camp, and no knowledge of where he was to be sent, or if he would ever come back again. Well, at least this joy was his to keep and remember when he had nothing else.

So he met her with the same eagerness in his own face, and like two children they started out together for a sweet adventure.

"Now, where do we go?" asked Phil Pilgrim looking down at Laurel, with no idea how his eyes were admiring her.

"Oh," said Laurel, and looked down, suddenly embarrassed at what she was about to say. "Oh, I hope you won't mind. If you do it's all right, you know. I don't want to do it if you don't like it. Perhaps I hadn't any business to butt in on your affairs, and please don't let me do it if you would rather not—!"

Pilgrim turned a puzzled look toward her.

"But what is it? You haven't told me yet what you want to do."

"Oh!" laughed Laurel, "excuse me! I thought I had. Yes, I told you a long time ago, didn't I? Only I didn't ask you whether you would like it or not. I want you to take me up to your little cemetery and let me put some flowers beside those two white stones. Do you mind? Because it's all right if you'd rather not."

"Oh! my *dear!—friend!"* he added, catching his breath. "Why should you think I would rather not? You could not do anything that would please me better than to put this thoughtful human touch of flowers out on those two lonely graves. I can't thank you enough for planning it, and I am so glad you let me be in on it enough to take you up there. It is beautiful, and I'll never forget it."

"Oh, I'm glad!" said Laurel, relief dawning in her face. "After I got the flowers and started to meet you I was just afraid you wouldn't like it, that it might hurt you somehow, and I couldn't bear the thought of that, after you have been so good to me."

"I think a man would be a brute not to like such a thing. I am more touched than I shall ever be able to show you. It means a great deal to me."

They said very little more as they drove up the mountain, the pleasant way, by the smooth road. They passed the trail to the picnic ground, and then the old weather-beaten house where the Pilgrims had lived their dreary years, till they came to the little clearing by the roadside where stood the two white stones.

Pilgrim stopped the car, helped Laurel out, and brought her the box of flowers, from the back of the car.

He breathed a soft exclamation of wonder as she opened it. Such magnificence of bloom, such wealth of beauty, such soft delicate perfume as swept out to his senses. She had done it so perfectly. Not any showy flowers that could not harmonize with the thought of his little quiet plain grandmother, living her somber life away from the world. But those soft colors, minded one of little children around the throne of Heaven where the grandmother would be feeling at Home. And they brought the tears to the eyes of the grandson, who had been only a small lonely boy when she left the earth, and left her two boys, the old one and the young one, alone.

Laurel knelt on the ground, where autumn leaves made a royal carpet, and took the flowers from the box, a few at a time, laying them over the bare mounds on their glossy leaves, until the whole was covered. And for once the stark place was filled with beauty, reminding one of a resurrection time when the two beneath the earth should rise with new life.

They stayed there motionless for a moment, and the light of the slowly sinking sun touched the flowers with ruby and rose and gave an unearthly beauty to the place. Laurel was kneeling, laying the last roses in place, and Pilgrim stood beside her, his head bowed reverently, his eyes on the girl who had done this lovely thing, his lips as if a prayer were forming on them.

Then Laurel spoke, shyly, softly, and the young man came nearer to hear her.

"Dear Father in Heaven, we believe that these two dear ones who are lying here are in Thy tender care. Please give them peace, and if it be possible let them know we have thought about them lovingly. And please help us, and take care of Phil Pilgrim as he goes back to camp. Amen."

She was very still for a moment afterward, kneeling with closed eyes. And then as she opened them there were tears on her face, and tears on the face of the young man as he lifted her to her feet.

So they stood close together for a little, his hand reaching out and holding hers softly. And suddenly she began to sing in a sweet clear voice, yet softly as an angel might have chanted:

Peace, perfect peace, with loved ones far away?
In Jesus' keeping we are safe and they.

As the melody swept out softly, Pilgrim joined in with a low accompaniment that was scarcely more than a hum, and as they sang together his hold on her hand grew closer and hers clung to his. They were both thinking about their dear ones who had gone from them. This was a little service for them.

Laural did not know all the verses, but the ones that came to mind she sang:

Peace, perfect peace, our future all unknown?
Jesus we know, and He is on the throne.

Just a moment more they stood in that quiet evening silence, with the sun sinking lower and lower, and the rosy light still on the flowers, and reflected in the sweet gravity of their faces. Then hand in hand they walked back to the car, the silence only broken by the sharp chirp of a cricket near by, the raucous caw of a blackbird in the top of a tall tree.

"I am glad you did that," said Pilgrim in a voice husky with feeling as they drove slowly down from Crimson Mountain. "It was like a service. And there wasn't any service for Grandfather. There was a minister for Grandmother when she died, but he had moved away before Grandfather died, and I was only a kid. I didn't know where to get one for Grandfather. Anyhow the undertaker was in a hurry to get done and go. So there wasn't any. But this would do for them both."

"Oh," said Laurel sorrowfully. "I'm glad you thought it was all right. I hadn't planned that. It just came to me that we ought to say something to God about it."

"It was beautiful!" said Pilgrim solemnly. "I kept thinking about some words Grandmother used to be saying. They began, 'Let not your heart be troubled—' but I couldn't remember the rest."

"Oh, yes, I know," said Laurel. "I learned that whole chapter once. It's the fourteenth of John. 'Let not your heart be troubled, ye believe in God, believe also in me.' "

"Yes, that's it," said Pilgrim. "I'm glad you remembered it. Where did you say that was? I might like to read it sometimes."

"I'll find it for you," said Laurel reaching her hand for the Testament he brought out, and fluttering through the leaves skillfully.

She handed the book back and he read the words again.

"Only," he said after an instant's thoughtful pause, "*do* we believe in God? If we don't we haven't any right to that comfort, have we? What does that mean, exactly, anyway?"

"I don't think I quite know," said Laurel thoughtfully. "I know my mother loved that verse and that chapter, and I'm sure my mother and father both believed in God. Don't you?"

"Perhaps," said Pilgrim. "I'm not sure. But I don't suppose that kind of believing is enough, is it?"

"I never thought about it that way," said Laurel. "It might be worth taking thought about."

They were very quiet, as they drove down old Crimson till they were almost at the foot of the road again, and then Pilgrim asked her:

"How about going to make that call on Mrs. Gray now? Or shall we go to the tea room first and have dinner? There won't be many people there now you know."

"That's a good idea," said Laurel. "Let's get dinner first and then make our call. Unless you had something else you wanted to do this evening."

"No indeed. I'm at your service, and only too glad to have company on what would otherwise be a lonely time. And by the way, I'm not going back to camp till late Monday afternoon. It develops that I'm needed to go up to Crimson and make sure about some boundary lines on Monday. Also I'm arranging to keep the cemetery lot for the present too. I'm glad for that. I wouldn't like to have that destroyed right away after that sacred hour we spent there with the flowers."

She flashed a look of appreciation at him.

"Oh, I'm glad you feel that way too," she said softly. "And now tell me about your land. Is it truly sold? And did the lawyer succeed in getting more for it than Mr. Banfield offered?"

"He certainly did. You'd be surprised. I was. And so was Mr. Banfield. Yes, the land is sold all right, and all I have left to do is to go up Crimson Monday morning with the surveyors and show them where the linefence marks are."

"Isn't that grand! Are you pleased, or do you feel just the least bit sorry to see it go?" asked Laurel.

"No, not even a little bit sorry," said Pilgrim grimly. "My grandfather had to take that land over from a man who owed him a lot of money and never even tried to pay him, and it came at a time when he was too deeply in debt, and worn with worry and sickness, to make anything of it in profit. It came, too, when Grandmother ought to have been in a warmer climate, and couldn't go because there wasn't money to finance a change. Nobody would buy it for even a song then, and we had no money for fertilizers to make the land a success, even if Grandfather had been able for farm work. I would gladly have pitched in and worked on the farm myself, but Grandfather wouldn't let me. He insisted I must have an education, and he almost gave his life to give me one. You see that land represents unhappiness and hardship for the people I loved, so I am glad it is sold at last. I have a feeling that if they are where they can know anything about what happens on the earth that they are glad too."

"I am sure they are," said Laurel. "I never really put the idea into words, but I often felt that my mother and father knew about what I was doing, and were glad for certain things that came to me."

He watched the changing expressions on her face, and wondered again how it was that he should have fallen in with a girl like this. A girl from the aristocratic walks of life who yet could talk simply and seriously of life and make it mean something besides personal gain and trifling amusement.

They talked a little about the war, and the possibility of raids reaching their own land, and whether the troops from America would be sent abroad. They grew grave over what would be happening to Pilgrim's company when he got back to camp, and Laurel suddenly realized that she was talking to this young man with a feeling that somebody very near and intimate with her was a part of this great war, that hitherto had touched her but in a distant thought. Oh, there were several of the men she knew who were in the army, most of them officers, and in a position of favor. They were wealthy young men who knew how to use influence to work for their favor. It had all seemed very light and unlikely that they would ever reach a real place of battle. But this young man was different. He was not seeking to evade danger, nor elude duty. He was not seeking high places nor selfish gain in the affairs of the world. He took his duty seriously, and was even laying aside his ambitions, and surrendering his life goal to serve the cause of right in its stern crisis. It thrilled her to think of it, while it yet drew her anxiety for him, and her admiration for his attitude.

The tea room was beginning to fill up fast now for the evening meal, as they loitered through their dinner. But suddenly they remembered that it was getting late, and they had planned to make a call.

Reluctantly they drew their conversation to an abrupt close and arose, realizing that the time of their separation was rapidly drawing nearer. Who could tell whether there would yet be time for any more talking after this?

DO you know," said Pilgrim as he helped her into the car, "Mark has fixed up my old jalopy so well that I think I'm taking it back to camp with me, in the hope that I can either get some use out of it down there, or else find a better sale for it in case I have to leave the country soon."

"Oh," said Laurel with a little catch in her breath, that sounded like dismay. And then just in time, she added coolly, "But of course, if you have to leave the country you would want to sell it. Still if you don't leave it will be nice for you to keep it to come back now and then if you have the chance."

"Yes," said Pilgrim, "I would need it in that case," and he sighed a little wearily as if he had but small hope of any such possibility.

Then they drew up in front of a little white bungalow with sturdy evergreens nestled about its porch, and a bright light shining from pleasant windows with frail diaphanous curtains of white.

"Oh, what a sweet little home," said Laurel eagerly. "Did she live here when you were a boy?"

"Yes, she's always been right here. I think somebody told me she came here as a bride. It certainly is a swell little house, and the little lady looks just as if she belonged here. As if the house was built around her to suit her every need."

"What a description!" laughed Laurel. "See, you have prejudiced me in her favor even before I have seen her."

"Well, I know you'll like her, and I'm sure she will like you. I sort of wanted you to have someone that I knew to whom you could go now and then," and he gave her a shy smile. "Of course it's none of my business, you know, and I don't want to presume."

"But you're not presuming. It will be wonderful to know a friend of yours."

"Oh, but now, maybe I have given you a wrong impression," he said anxiously. "You know she wouldn't count herself a personal *friend* of mine. One doesn't make personal friends of the boy who delivers eggs and berries, but she was nice to me many times, went out of her way to be nice, and I'm sure she would take my word for it what you are. You see with you it would be different. She probably knows your family—"

"Oh, now, please don't begin that kind of talk," said Laurel determinedly, "we're just friends, and no different at all. If your lady is what you say she is she won't have any ideas like that. She wouldn't *want* you to have an inferiority complex you know. If she did she wouldn't be fine as you say she is. She would laugh at such an idea. We have to stand on our own merits, not on how much money our parents had when they died. If she is going to make a distinction between us on that kind of a basis I don't want to go in."

"All right, you win," said Pilgrim with a grin. "Come on, let's go in and you can judge for yourself what she is."

So they walked together up the white steps, passing

between the evergreens to where a bright brass knocker shone on a very white door. Pilgrim boldly put out his hand and knocked, conscious all the time that the last time he went to that little house he had gone to the back door, and not to the front.

A sweet little woman came to the door, soft wavy brown hair with threads of silver tucked back smoothly, coiled low in her neck. Steady, kind blue eyes, a gentle, firm, pleasant mouth, trim little figure almost like a girl's, fine intelligent hands with steady purpose in their motions.

Pilgrim stepped forward, almost shyly, the old days suddenly upon his memory.

"Mrs. Gray, I'm Phil Pilgrim. Have you forgotten me?"

The keen blue eyes went to his face and studied it a moment.

"Phil Pilgrim!" she said, and a light came into her face. "Phil Pilgrim! So it is! You went away to college! I heard about it! And now you're a soldier boy! I'm proud of you!"

Her hands went out in welcome, as if he had been some one closely related to her. She took his hands in a warm quick clasp, and then her eyes went to Laurel, as she stood in the shadow looking on with deep interest.

"And this is—your—?" she looked at Pilgrim for explanation.

"This is a friend, Miss Sheridan. Maybe you know her too, Mrs. Gray. She used to live here. At least you must have known *of* her."

The keen eyes turned with quick scrutiny, and lit up with a new welcome.

"Sheridan!" she said. "Sheridan? Not Langdon Sheridan's daughter?"

"Yes," said Pilgrim eagerly, "she is. I thought you would know the Sheridans."

The blue eyes lit up again.

"I certainly did," said Mrs. Gray, putting out her hands and taking both of Laurel's in a warm folding. "Your mother was a wonderful woman, my dear. I admired her so much. She went to the same Bible-study class I did, and we often looked over the same hymn book together. She was president of our Ladies' Aid, and did so many lovely things for other people. She was a dear woman. Of course she didn't know me very well, though she was always so cordial when we met, and made me feel that I was one of her best friends. And your father was a great man. I shall never forget how many wonderful things he did quietly to help just plain insignificant people. Come in, my dear. I'm honored to have you here. Come in, Philip. It's nice of you to have looked me up."

They followed the little lady into her sweet quiet home that looked so livable and pleasant, and sat down, both feeling happy to be with her.

"Oh, I'm so glad you knew my dear mother, and my father," said Laurel.

"You look like your mother, my dear," said Mrs. Gray. "She was a beautiful woman. You should be proud to look like her."

"Oh, I am. It is good that you think I am like her. I shall enjoy knowing you so much, I am sure. I shall be so glad if you will be my friend."

"Why of course, my dear. I'll love to be that. But I thought you had moved away somewhere. I haven't heard that any of the Sheridan family were left in this part of the world."

"She's just come back to try living here," explained Pilgrim. "She felt rather alone and I told her I thought she would enjoy knowing you. You had always been so good to me I dared to bring her here."

"Well, that's beautiful," said Mrs. Gray. "And I shall

be so glad if she will come often to see me. You know I'm going to be very lonesome this winter. My nephew who has been living with me since his wife died has gone to Canada and joined the British army. He is already in England now, and so I am entirely alone. I'll just love having company. And now, Phil, tell me all about yourself, your college, what you did, and where you are going, now you are a soldier."

Pilgrim gave her a nice grin.

"Thanks for your interest," he said. "I graduated all right. Did some athletic work and other things to help me through financially, and the next thing of course was to join the army. It seemed to be the right thing to do. Of course naturally it wasn't just what I would have *chosen* to come next in life after I finished college, but it had to be, because war didn't consult me when it decided to come our way. So I enlisted. My camp is down in Virginia just now, but there is likelihood we'll be moved in a few days."

"You're home for the week end? A furlough?"

"Not exactly." said Pilgrim. "I got word the government wanted to buy my land for a munitions factory, and I got leave to come home and go through the formalities of the sale."

"You don't say! Now that's interesting, isn't it? But don't you hate to give up the old home?"

"No," said Pilgrim, a cloud coming over the brightness of his face. "I never had any love for it. The folks are all dead you know, and there wasn't much joy ever up there."

"Yes, I remember," the dear little woman sighed sympathetically. "Well, then it's nice that you could sell it."

"I thought so," said Pilgrim.

Then the lady turned to Laurel.

"And now, tell me about you. Are you just here visiting, or are you coming back to live?"

"No, I'm not visiting," said Laurel. "I have a job. Of course I'm not sure how long it will last, or whether I can fill it. I'm to start Monday teaching in the high school where a teacher was sick and has gone to California."

"Oh, my dear. Then you are going to be here. How fortunate for me! Then I may really hope to see you this winter. At least until you get into the life of the town, I suppose."

"I don't believe there is any life in this town that would keep me from visiting the new friend I think you look as if you might be."

"You sweet child! And so you're going to teach in the high school! What fortunate scholars to have a girl like you for their teacher!"

And so they talked on, getting better and better acquainted, and finally Mrs. Gray turned to Pilgrim.

"Philip, did you say you are going to be here over Sunday?"

"Yes. I can't leave till I have been up to the place to meet the engineers about the dividing lines. They want me to help locate the original surveyors' marks. It may take some time."

"Oh, I see," said Mrs. Gray. "Well, I'm glad you're staying, for I thought it would be nice if you two were to take dinner with me tomorrow just to sort of cement our friendship, and as a reminder of the days when you were a little boy and I knew you. Could you both do that?" She turned her glance from Pilgrim's face to the sweet face of the girl. "Or had you both some other plan for the day, Miss Sheridan? Perhaps some of your old friends have already asked you? I don't want to be selfish, of course."

Laurel laughed a sweet ripple of a laugh.

"My old friends, if there are any of them left here, don't even know I have come back. No, I haven't a thing to do tomorrow but to get through the day in a strange boarding house, so *I'll* be just delighted to come, whatever Phil does."

"Oh, I wouldn't miss it for anything!" said Pilgrim with a look as if he had been invited into Heaven for a few hours.

"Well, that will be just perfect!" said Mrs. Gray, her eyes shining. "And say, I wonder if I dare go a little farther and ask you if you would mind coming over early enough to go to church with me? Do you know, I always feel so lonely going to church alone since my nephew left me. It would be nice to have a couple of dear young people with me. And I kind of think you will enjoy the sweet simple little church where I go. It isn't a great church, and they are not many of them wealthy, but they love the Lord, and I think you couldn't help seeing how genuine they are."

"Why of course we'll go with you, Mrs. Gray," said Laurel earnestly. "That is—" and she suddenly looked toward Pilgrim, *"I'll* be glad to go. I can't answer for Mr. Pilgrim. I don't know what his engagements are."

"Engagements!" grinned Pilgrim. "If I were unfortunate enough to have any hindering engagements I would certainly cancel them. I'll be here, Mother Gray, right on the dot. Will ten o'clock be time enough?"

"Oh, *surely!*" said the smiling lady. "And I'm as happy as a bird to think you are coming with me. Now, don't hurry!—" as the two young people arose, "can't you wait long enough to eat a few cookies? Philip, you used to like my cookies."

"I sure did! They were swell!"

"And I'm just eager to taste them," laughed Laurel.

A little while and they were on their way again. True, they had no other place to go, but both of them felt that they had had a reprieve. Strange, thought Laurel, that she should feel this way about a friend whom she had just picked out of the blue as it were. Of course he was all right. She remembered having seen him when he was a boy. He remembered her. She had heard of his success in college. He had demonstrated to her that he had respectable friends, and his behavior to her had been irreproachable. She had no trouble in her heart about that. Her only concern was that she should so soon have developed this great interest in him, and that she should feel so unreasonably happy to think they were to have one more day together.

"Well, how do you like her?" asked Phil Pilgrim after they had driven a couple of blocks away from the little white house.

"Oh, I think she's just *wonder*ful. Yes, Phil, she's all you said she was, and more. I just love her, and I'm so glad you took me there! It's going to make a big difference in my winter to have a friend like that."

"I thought maybe it would," said Pilgrim slowly, thoughtfully. "It's going to make me a lot happier about leaving you here alone." And then suddenly he grew red and hot in the darkness.

"Of course it's none of my business," he hurried to add. "I had no right to try and plan your life for you. With my few resources it was presumption in me. But I thought maybe she might help you out sometime in an emergency. She did that for me more than once."

"I see what you mean," said Laurel gently, "and I thank you with all my heart. I'm going to take a lot of pleasure knowing her. I think she's rare."

They drove on into a moonlit world, over some of the dear old road that both of them had known in their childhood, knitting up a friendship moment by moment that counted almost up to years before they turned and went back.

"I must get you home before it is noticeably late you know," said Phil Pilgrim with a grin. "Your first night in that new boarding place it wouldn't do for you to be out too late with an unknown soldier."

"Well, of course," said Laurel, "if we were coming from a night club somewhere nobody would think anything of it these days. But I'm glad you're taking care of me. It is what my mother would appreciate, and I guess it will be well for my reputation as a schoolmarm, too."

"Oh, I imagine so. But still, I don't suppose that would count much as yet. But by the way, how do you feel about that going-to-church business? Do you mind?"

"*Mind?* I think it's *lovely.* I like it. Why? Don't you?"

"Oh, yes! I like Mrs. Gray's way of looking at things. I never went to that place where she says she goes, but I'm sure it will be interesting. I don't suppose it's the church which your people attended."

"I don't care about that. But they must have gone to the same church when my mother was alive. Don't you know she spoke of being in the same Ladies' Aid and Missionary Society?"

"That's true. But Mrs. Gray is one who would help out a new work if she thought it worthy. Still we'll see. The big church may have grown too worldly to please her. A good many churches seem to have got that way these days."

"Yes, I know," said Laurel seriously. "I haven't been going to church much lately. Somehow the ones I chanced on didn't seem to mean much. They were just eager about how many came, and how much money they raised."

"Yes, that's the way they impressed me," said Pilgrim. "I couldn't seem to get anything out of them. Perhaps I didn't find the right ones. But lately, since I went to camp, I've been going to the meetings we have there. There's a crackerjack chaplain down there, and he seems to be real as far as I can find out. He talks about being 'saved' as if it was something you could be sure of. I don't know. If all Christians were like that I might take stock in it. Maybe I'll have time to think it over while I'm in the army. Seems like a thing one ought to take some thought about if one is going out to possibly be shot you know."

"Oh, don't talk that way," said Laurel with a sudden shiver, "*please* don't!" She laid her hand gently on his arm for an instant.

"Why! Would *you* care?" he asked, looking down at her in a kind of wonder.

"Yes! Yes, of course," she said with almost a sob. "Of course I would care. You saved my life! And you've been wonderful to me. Don't spoil this lovely day by talking about being shot."

He was very still for a moment and then he said, "Thank you for that. I never really thought about anybody caring what would happen to me!"

And then they suddenly arrived at the boarding house, with lights blazing forth from over the front door, and from most of the windows. Three young men were getting out of a car in front of them and marching up the walk to the steps.

Laurel suddenly looked up and recognized the shoulders of two of those young men, and drew back into the car out of sight, clutching fiercely the hand that still held hers.

"Oh, do I have to go in there just yet?" she asked annoyedly. "Couldn't we drive on for a little? I don't want to go in there right in front of all those men."

"Of course we'll drive on a little farther," said Pilgrim, a ring of satisfaction in his voice. "It's only eleven o'clock yet. And where, by the way, did you arrange to keep your car?"

"Just around the corner there. It's only a step. There's a way out the back gate."

"I see," said Pilgrim, "that's not so bad. Suppose we drive around a block or two and watch when their car goes away. I might get a glimpse of those men and see if I know any of them."

"I thought *I* did," said Laurel in a small voice.

"You *did?* Are they men you know and can trust?"

"I know them—I guess," said Laurel. "That is I've met them in the city among my cousin's friends. But they are not my kind of people. I would rather not meet them just now, anyway. They know nothing about my life, and would only laugh and jeer at my trying to earn a living. They are people who like to play a lot. They don't take life seriously. Anyway, I'd rather not see them at present. About trusting them, I wouldn't know. I never had to. They are pleasant enough, and polite, at a party. That is all I've seen of them. One was a war correspondent in Germany until a short time ago. His name is Winter. I'm not sure but the other one was a writer too. His name is Rainey."

"I see," said Pilgrim thoughtfully. "Now, what could we do about this? Would you rather get a room at the tea room for tonight? Do you dislike meeting them as much as that?"

"I couldn't," said Laurel. "All my things are locked in my room. No, of course it's not as important as that. I just would rather be forgotten. They don't need to know where I am. Unless of course they are staying here for awhile. Then I couldn't very well help myself. But maybe they only dropped in to see somebody and will go on pretty soon."

"Perhaps," he said. "We'll see."

So they drove around for a little longer, too much under the spell of their recent words, and the silver night, to make much conversation. Perhaps, too, a little occupied with the thought of the intruding men. Phil Pilgrim was troubled that his companion of the day was planning to abide in a house that was open to strange boarders. It was no place for her to be staying.

He spoke out his thought presently.

"I know," said Laurel. "It may not be as pleasant as I would like, but perhaps I'd better try it out. The room is very pleasant and convenient. There is an upper porch opening off it that attracted me."

"But I don't like to leave you in a place like that. You seem so unprotected."

"Thank you. It's nice to think someone cares," she smiled. "But you see I took the room for a week, and left a deposit. I think I had better try to stay if possible and see what it's like. Of course if those men are the ones I know they are quite all right as far as safety is concerned. But they are just not the kind I care to choose for intimates. And I imagine it would be hard to live in the close-quarters of a boarding house without a certain degree of intimacy."

"Rather!" said Pilgrim dryly. She had never had much experience of boarding houses, and he had, and spoke out of his wider knowledge.

"I feel," he said, with slow hesitation, "as if I were somehow responsible for you, and I don't like to go far away and leave you in a place that I am not perfectly sure about."

He looked down at her through the moonlight, and an answer of utter trust and confidence flashed between them.

And just then they turned again into the street of the boarding house, and saw two of the men, the two that Laurel thought she knew, coming out of the house, while the third stood at the top of the steps and waved a hand as in farewell.

The two men who looked like Winter and Rainey came out to their car and hurriedly drove away in the direction they would take if they were returning to the city. The third man went back in, and as they drew up before the house they could see him mounting the stairs with his suitcase.

"Well, thank goodness, that hazard is past for the night anyway," said Laurel. "I don't know why I was such a silly about those two men. They were nice enough, even quite attentive, and I didn't dislike them. I just didn't want to have the whole mob of people I left behind me find out where I am and come howling after me every time they have a party or anything. I don't want to live their kind of life, and they can make it mighty uncomfortable for me if they find out where I am right now at the beginning, especially if they go back and get Cousin Carolyn started after me. But I suppose that is foolish. If I take a stand and stick to it they'll soon learn."

"I understand," said Pilgrim with a soft little touch of reassurance on the hand that lay next to him on the seat.

"Thank you," said the girl happily. "I sort of knew you would. And now, shall we put the car in the garage? I have the key of my cubby hole here. And then I can slip in the side door of the house."

He put the car away for her and walked with her to the side door.

"Suppose you meet me in front of the tea room at nine-thirty in the morning. Will that be too early?" he said quietly.

"That will be quite all right for me," she answered in a whisper, "and thanks for everything—all day!"

He grasped her hand giving it a quick little pressure and then he brought it swiftly up to his lips and laid them reverently upon it.

"Good night," he said, and opened the door for her, disappearing quickly into the shadows of the path.

Laurel went hurriedly into the office and asked for her key of the sleepy clerk who was lolling in a big chair with a movie magazine. She was thankful that there was no one else in the office. She accomplished the distance to her own room without meeting anyone and was glad when the door was locked between herself and the world, and she could sit down for a minute and take in the thought of those lips upon her hand. What had come over her that a thing like that should produce such a tumult in her breast? She had had her hand kissed before, but not like this. Not with such reverence, such tenderness! There was a quality to that caress that went deep into her soul, stirred her almost to tears, as if she had unexpectedly found something great and dependable. Somehow the experiences of yesterday and today had changed her outlook on life, and it would never be the same again.

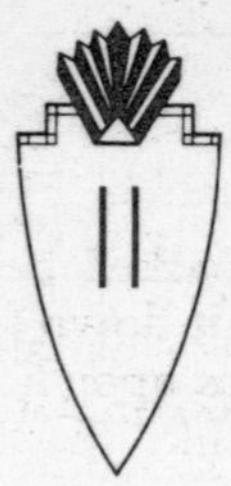

SUNDAY morning when Laurel awoke she found her room flooded with sunshine. It was really a very pleasant room. Two windows looked toward Crimson Mountain, its glorious blending of color plainly visible. After all, perhaps this was as good a boarding place as she could find.

The breakfast was fairly good, though Laurel was not critical this particular morning. She was full of the anticipation of the day, her mind dwelling on little things that had been said and done the day before. That reverent kiss on her fingers, nothing silly about it the way so many people of the world fooled around with kissing. It was almost a homage done her, and it stirred her even in memory more than she had yet owned to herself. This was the most interesting young man she had ever yet met. Were there others like him? He seemed so different. Oh, perhaps she was just silly and would snap out of it pretty soon, but she was enjoying it all and didn't want to miss a single minute of this lovely day that was before her.

She had the dining room almost to herself, for the

other boarders, if any, had not chosen to arise so early. There was just one young man over at the table in the corner, eating stolidly with downcast eyes. He was thickset, low-browed, broad shouldered, with large hands, blunt fingers and small sharp eyes. Twice she had a feeling that he was looking at her and glancing up involuntarily at him she caught his sharp eyes boring into her, as if he were trying to pierce through her personality, but as she turned away his eyes seemed to fade out like a moving picture, as if they had not been lifted at all. Yet she knew they had. It was uncanny. She had a distinct photographic vision on her own retina of how those eyes had looked, like ruthless gimlets boring into her life and examining it. She didn't like it. It was weird. She felt as if he had torn away all reserve in herself, examined every cranny of her soul, and would be able now to understand everything she did. Oh, she didn't want to be near him! Maybe it was silly, but definitely, if he was going to be a regular boarder here she would find some other place. And she would do it so unobtrusively that he would never find out where she was gone, if that was possible.

She brought her breakfast to a hasty finish and went out to the office to inform the landlady that she would not be at dinner that day.

"Oh, all right," said that person, studying her almost insolently. "Well, I was going to tell you that you can't count meals out unless I have plenty of notice beforehand. Two days if possible. They have to be paid for whether they're et or not. Understand?"

"Yes?" said Laurel lifting her eyebrows amusedly. "Well, all right. That seems fair enough. I'll remember."

The landlady pursed her lips offendedly and prepared another economic blast.

"Well, I'm glad you understand that point. And now there's another. You said you weren't sure about taking your room for the winter, and I just wanted to let you know that I've had an application for it. It seems that's true about the big munition works gonto be built here in this neighborhood, and that means housing conditions are going to be crowded. I had three men come in last night and they wanted the three rooms. They just left a few minutes before you come in. That is two of them did. The other man stayed and is here now. They wanted the three rooms together, and liked yours best of all. They will take them for the winter, so if you wantta keep that room you took you'll have ta give me an answer at once or run the risk of losing it altogether. I couldn't afford ta lose a rent fer the winter, just fer one week's rent."

"I beg your pardon, Mrs. Price. I understood that you rented me the room for a week, and accepted a down payment with that idea in mind. Are you telling me that you would like me to leave tonight?"

"I didn't say that. I'm only saying I can't afford to let a chance go fer renting the room fer the winter in case you decide not to stay. But that wasn't saying you hadta leave tanight. I just want a quick decision."

"I can't possibly give you a decision tomorrow," said Laurel firmly. "I may have time to look around further on Monday afternoon but I'm not sure. If you are in as much of a hurry as that I had better get my things and go elsewhere tonight, and you can refund me the money I gave you."

Mrs. Price gave a quick little gasp.

"Oh, no, I ain't in as much of a hurry as that. Of course you can stay till Tuesday, or mebbe Wednesday if nobody else don't come in a hurry and want your room right away."

"All right, Mrs. Price. I wanted to try out this location and see whether it suits me in every respect before I take the room indefinitely, but since you have other renters waiting I'll see what I can do about a decision as much before the week is up as possible."

Laurel spoke coolly, and decidedly, and Mrs. Price began to hedge a little. She didn't want to lose this good-looking girl. With a lot of young men in the place, such a girl would be an asset.

"Well, I'll do me best for ye," she called after the girl as she mounted the stairs to get ready to meet Phil Pilgrim. But the landlady looked after her with a bit of worry on her brow. Had she gone the least bit too far in endeavoring to make a profitable deal with this toploftical young woman?

But Laurel did not stop to talk further. She marched on to her room, and was soon ready for the day, thankful that there was still bright sunshine.

She looked very pretty as she came down the stairs a few minutes later, dressed in a blue suit that just matched her eyes, and a little hat that was most becoming. Mrs. Price looked after her worriedly and thought again that as good-looking a young woman as that ought to be a great attraction in a boarding house where there would likely be a lot of young men coming. Maybe she would try to make her a little better offer after all, when she came back. Then she heard the girl's car driving out of the garage, and turned with a sigh to answer that new Mr. Byrger's questions about how far it was to the top of Crimson Mountain.

That was a notable day to both the young people who drove off together to get their hostess and take her to church.

In the first place the church was different from any church that Phil Pilgrim or Laurel had ever attended. They felt the atmosphere as they entered the door.

It was not a large handsome church. Just a little old-fashioned place that had the air of a good many years ago. The carpet was worn, the seats were a bit narrow and hard, and the windows wore no stained glass. But everything was clean and attractive, and the sun was shining in across the heads of the people, touching them with a sort of glory-look, and there seemed to be loving kindness in every face. The two young people sat down and looked about them wonderingly. What was it that made this simple gathering so different from other worshiping places? It seemed as if God were there. As if they could almost see Him, if they could only get the earth mist brushed away from their eyes.

And then the singing! They were not cultured voices, but they had the sweetness and heartiness of voices that were singing from the heart. They both joined in and began to feel a thrill of belonging to this little company of worshipers, worshiping in spirit and in truth.

The minister was young almost like themselves, but he spoke with the deep conviction of one who believed with all his soul what he was saying, and it seemed that all the congregation had brought their Bibles. Someone stepped across the aisle and handed the two young strangers Bibles from a pile in the end of the seat, and they took them and turned over the pages. Laurel had no trouble in finding the places, but Phil Pilgrim looked furtively over his shoulder at Laurel's Bible to see in which end of the book she had located the place. Phil Pilgrim was evidently not accustomed to looking up references in the Bible. But as he listened to the amazing truth that the young speaker was bringing out from the references they all read together he began to be intensely interested. He had never heard anybody try to explain the Bible, not since he was a little boy at his mother's knee, and that was so long ago, and so very elementary. He wondered if his girl-mother had ever known these things were in the Bible, or had she just read it as a sort of duty? And was it possible that these things were maybe being explained in Heaven to those who hadn't fully understood while they lived on earth? But it was foolish to reason that way. Perhaps his mother had known more than she had been able to teach him because he was so small.

At the close of service the kindly people gathered around and welcomed the young strangers, and Pilgrim told the young minister that he only wished he were going to be in Carrollton this winter. He certainly would like to accept the invitation so cordially given and come again, many times.

Driving home to Mrs. Gray's, Pilgrim was very quiet, half listening as Mrs. Gray and Laurel talked, Laurel asking questions about people she used to know in town. Suddenly Mrs. Gray turned to Pilgrim:

"Well, how did you like our little church, Phil?" she asked.

Pilgrim turned his steady eyes toward her.

"It's a wonderful place, Mrs. Gray. I wish I were able to stay here and go every Sunday to a place like that. I never knew there could be as much real help gotten out of anything in the Bible as that. I shan't forget this morning's sermon. It wasn't like any sermon I ever heard. It was like a study. It left me with the same kind of thrill I used to get when some new fact of science was brought out in a class in college. Only that would have to do with physical things, but the sermon this morning was about spiritual things. And I don't believe I ever heard spiritual things analyzed before. It's interesting. I like it. I wish I could hear more."

"Yes," said Ellen Gray with a happy gleam in her quiet eyes, "it is good to study those things. To find out that there is a spiritual world as well as a natural one, and that the spiritual one is the real one, the one that is to last forever, while the physical world will pass away. You see that is the reason that I have left the old church, the one your mother and I used to attend when you were a little girl," she said, turning to Laurel with a smile. "They got a minister over there about three years ago who laughs at the idea of anybody believing the whole of the Bible, and who won't let them have an evening Bible class one night in the week because the man we wanted to teach it is 'too radical' he says. But my soul was hungry for the truth. I got to thinking that the time of my going from this earth was drawing nearer and nearer, and I didn't rightly understand a great many things in God's Word, so I heard about this place and I came over here a few times and found great refreshment. I'm glad you liked it. I thought you would. And now here we are. I must hurry in and look after the dinner I left cooking. You young people take your time coming in. It will be a half hour before dinner is on the table."

Mrs. Gray opened the car door and slipped out to the sidewalk before Pilgrim could get there to help her and was unlocking her door and into the house like a flash.

"Isn't she sweet?" said Laurel earnestly. "And wasn't that a wonderful service? I haven't heard anything that seemed to reach what I was really thinking in my heart before, about—well, you know—Heaven, and the hereafter."

Pilgrim nodded.

"Yes, that's what I mean. I never heard anybody talk in that definite way before about being saved. I thought that was something you couldn't know about, even if you did your best to live a right kind of a life, until after you were dead."

"Oh, I knew better than that," said Laurel, who was listening earnestly. "I knew that there was a way to be saved, and that you could find that way if you wanted to enough. One of the verses I learned when I was a little girl was 'And ye shall find me when ye shall seek for me *with all your heart!*' But I'm afraid I never sought with all my heart. I was too interested in the things of this world really to pay enough attention to it, until later years when sorrow began to come along my way and I didn't know which way to turn. But even then I have been too much engaged in planning a tolerable life to take the place of the one I was losing, to give much thought to Eternal life. But I did know there was a way, and I definitely knew that my mother and my father both knew it. I have always intended sometime just to take time off and give attention to it, but I haven't ever done it yet."

They got out of the car and went slowly up the walk talking, opening up a doorway into their innermost thoughts. Laurel had never met anyone else to whom she could talk in this way. It was a revelation to find one who understood, and had had such thoughts himself. It forged another link in the chain of their acquaintance that was growing moment by moment into something that could never be easily broken.

In the house they followed out into the kitchen to see if there wasn't something they could do toward helping with the dinner, but they found Mrs. Gray had it all in hand. She was just lifting out the roasted lamb, with the beautifully roasted potatoes surrounding it, and taking up the perfectly cooked lima beans from a double boiler.

"Yes," she said briskly, "Phil, you may get the three plates of tomato salad from the refrigerator, and carry in the roast and potatoes, and then come back for the dish of beans. There's the cover to the dish. You'll find the table is all set."

Then turning to the girl she said:

"You may go to the refrigerator and get the butter. It's on a plate there, and the little pitcher of cream, also the pitcher of ice water. I got it ready before I went to church. You'll find the bread plate in that little tin cabinet in the pantry. The bread is all cut. I knew you'd be hungry when you got home from church. Now, I'll make the gravy and finish the coffee. I turned on the percolator the minute I came in."

It was just fun hurrying about under such able direction getting that delicious-looking meal on the table, laughing and talking as they worked.

Phil Pilgrim didn't need to be told to bring in the percolator and the gravy boat when they were ready, and Laurel had discovered the three pieces of pumpkin pie, the plate of delicate cheese cut in small inviting squares, the plates of pickles and olives and celery. In almost no time at all they were sitting down to the table.

And then there was an unexpected moment, when Mrs. Gray bowed her head.

It had been sometime since Laurel had been in a household where the custom of asking a blessing at the table was observed, but she fell into it naturally again, and it was sweet to hear the tender blessing.

"Lord, we thank Thee for this fellowship together, and we ask Thee to be a guest at our board, and to make Thy presence felt among us. We thank Thee also for these gifts that Thou hast given us. May they strengthen us for our life, and make our lives fit for Thy service. We ask it in Jesus' Name, Amen."

Then quite simply as if this had not been an innovation, the hostess went on to talk of the day and the service they had attended that morning, and all in the same spirit, Phil Pilgrim presently asked a question:

"Mrs. Gray, I've been wondering. Do you think a person can really know while they are living that they are saved? Your preacher spoke of people who were 'saved' as if it were something you could know beyond the shadow of a doubt."

"Why surely," said Mrs. Gray smiling.

"You *do?*" said Pilgrim. "Well *how* do you know? What do you have to do to get that assurance?"

"Why just take the Lord at His word, accept what He says, and then go on trusting in that and let Him prove it to you."

Pilgrim looked at her with a puzzled frown.

"Do you mean to say God promises a thing like that? Where? How?"

"Well, there are a great many places in the Bible where He has promised salvation, and assurance beyond a doubt. Perhaps the best known is John 3:16: 'For God so loved the world that He gave His only begotten Son, that whosoever believeth on Him should not perish, but have everlasting life.' But there are many many others. Take the book of John and begin to read it, looking for such promises. See how many you will come across."

"But do you mean believing saves you? Just *believing?* And how can you believe if you do not *know* it is so?"

"Yes, believing is the condition of salvation. That does not mean just an intellectual acknowledgment that Jesus once lived on this earth and once died on the cross. It means that you believe and *accept* what He came to earth to do for you. You and all of us were under condemnation of death for our sin and Jesus Christ came and took our sin upon Himself, as if He had Himself committed it, and bore the penalty in our stead, so that we might go free, and in the eyes of God be no longer under condemnation. But though He has done all that for us, it does us no good unless we *accept* it, *believe* it, and take Him for our personal Saviour. It all rests on that."

"You mean that's *all* we have to do?"

"Yes, that's all."

"But, I suppose you mean after that you have to live a perfect life, don't you?"

"No," said the lady gravely, "because you *couldn't* even if you tried with all your might. You still have that sinful nature as long as you live, and you could not of yourself live a perfect life. God did not leave us dependent on our own efforts for salvation because if He had none of us could be saved. The living part we do because we love Him, and want to please Him, and imperfect as it is, it pleases Him. But our best efforts never could save us. We have no plea to stand before the righteousness of a just God except that Jesus shed His blood to atone for our sin, and put His own righteousness about us after we accepted his atonement."

"I never heard it explained that way before," said Laurel. "You make it very plain, Mrs. Gray. I'm so glad I know you. Will you mind if I come and ask you questions sometimes?"

"Oh, I'd be delighted," said the little lady with sparkling eyes. "There is nothing I so enjoy as talking about the Lord, and studying His word with someone. Wouldn't you like to join our Bible study class Tuesday evenings?"

"I certainly would," said Laurel. "My mother loved to study her Bible, and I always wondered why, because when I tried to read it by myself it seemed dry and without point. I just couldn't understand it reading by myself. Of course I know a lot of general doctrines. That is I was taught them, but they never went deep into my understanding."

"But, I don't understand," said Phil Pilgrim. "Do you mean you just take statements in the Bible and go ahead and live by them as if they were proclamations, say from the government, or something like that?"

"I would put it rather that you take hold of *God's* statements and *believe* them. If you have God's word that you are saved, then nothing can touch you. You must take hold of God's promises. You must not question them. Believing is not something you do as a result of intellectual reasoning. It is accepting what you do not understand and putting it to its test afterward, as you might believe in a machine that would carry you somewhere, without understanding its mechanism. But once you trust yourself to it and let it carry you safely through, then your belief becomes knowledge. It is not *knowledge* of God that saves you, but *belief* that He has provided a way of salvation. It is taking Him and putting Him to trial in your life. As soon as you accept Christ as your personal Saviour, the Holy Spirit enters into your heart to guide you. You are born again, and a new joy begins to come to you as you become acquainted with the Lord Jesus Christ. When you know Him, you *know* you are saved. You no longer have any question about that."

They talked on while they ate the delicious dinner, asking questions and getting amazing answers in simple language that they could understand.

After a time they got up and helped Mrs. Gray clear off the table and wash the dishes, putting them carefully away again in their places. Then they adjourned to the pleasant living room and talked on, bringing forth all the questions that had arisen in their minds during their talk.

At last Mrs. Gray said:

"Are you two willing to accept Christ as your Saviour? You know it is not a thing that takes time. You can accept Him now, this minute and the thing is done. Will you?"

There was a moment of silence and then Pilgrim spoke:

"I will," he said definitely. "I need Him. I'm going into the war, and I want to get this thing settled at once. It's time I had something to rest upon, something to trust in. I can't just rest in what a gun can do for me, or my training as a soldier. I want God. I want to know that I am right with Him. Yes, I'll accept Him now."

"Yes, of course," said Laurel. "I want Him too. I need a Saviour. I think perhaps I did accept Him long ago when I was a little girl. I can remember my mother talking to me about it once. And my Sunday School teacher too. But I can't remember ever letting it make any difference in my life. But now I want to."

"Oh, my dear children," said the little lady Gray, tears of joy brightening her eyes. "Come, let us kneel down and tell Him so. It's just as easy as that!"

In the soft light of the setting sun they knelt together in the pleasant living room, while their hostess prayed a simple prayer for them, and then as she lingered for a moment on her knees Phil Pilgrim spoke:

"Oh Lord, I want to take You now as my Saviour. I don't know very much about it all yet, but I want to learn, and I'm accepting it and trusting You to take me, and to teach me what You want me to do. And—bless us *both!*"

Laurel's voice was clear and sweet as she followed.

"Oh, Lord Jesus Christ, I do now accept Thee as my Lord and Saviour. Teach me to do Thy will, and help me in the long way alone, for Jesus' sake."

When they arose there was a solemn joy in their faces, as if they somehow felt that the Lord had been right there beside them, making them sure that they were saved. And as they looked at one another the slowly sinking sun shot out a gorgeous light across the room upon them, like sudden glory, as if to crown what they had done. Then Phil Pilgrim quoted softly: "I gotta glory and I've got to live up to it." And he smiled to himself quietly as he saw the reflection of the same thought in the eyes of the lovely girl across the room.

They went to the evening church service. They were quite eager to go, and were as interested as any of the little earnest group in the chapel.

Then afterward Mrs. Gray made them come in with her again for toast and hot chocolate. And so it was quite late when they went back to the boarding house.

They put the car away in the garage, and then as they reached the side door where Laurel would naturally go in, Pilgrim drew her back from the steps.

"Let's just take a little walk around a block or two, shall we? I don't know whether I shall be able to see you much before I leave tomorrow. You have to go to school in the morning, don't you? What time?"

"I must be at the building a little before eight," she said, her voice almost sad.

"And I must meet the engineers very early," he said with something that sounded like a sigh.

Hand in hand they walked along the quiet street, Laurel's fingers held close, with something almost possessive in the grasp, or perhaps it would be better to say wistful, if fingers can express wistfulness. And the girl's hand nestled quietly in the boy's, thrilled at his touch. There were tears very near the surface and a feeling as if she were going to tremble. Silly of course, a girl about to be a schoolteacher, to feel this way at parting from a man she had only known two days! Yet they had been such precious days! Her fingers at the thought answered the pressure of his with a feeling too deep for mere words.

They walked around two or three blocks, coming into a quiet street where deep evergreens hedged the sidewalk, and their steps lagged more and more.

"Strange," he said in a low tone, "that we should know each other so well, as if it had been always!"

"I was just thinking that," murmured Laurel. "It doesn't seem as if I could let you go this way! Into war! How terrible life is sometimes!"

"Yes." He was still a long time, holding her hand closer. And then with a kind of a ring in his voice, "But we are both 'saved.' If the worst comes, there will be Heaven afterward. I never believed much in Heaven, but now somehow I do. It does make a difference to believe! I didn't expect a real difference, but there is. Do you feel it?"

"Yes. Oh yes. But anyway it isn't always *feel*ing I guess. To be saved means to be safe! And whether I feel it or not I *know* it is true. I've always known that, only I didn't let myself think about it."

He slipped her hand within his arm, and drew her closer to his side, comfortingly close, her hand still in his.

"I'm glad we found the Lord—together—today. At least—*you* used to know Him you say—but somehow our kneeling there together and binding ourselves to His service,—it seemed to make a tie—a sort of relationship we didn't have before! It made us both children of God, and where I had no right before I now can claim a relationship with you."

"Don't say you had no right before," said Laurel earnestly. "You *had* a right, the right of an old friend and schoolmate, and then the right of one who had saved my life, and been kind. Surely that was enough to offset the long years when we didn't know each other. And now—, yes, I see what you mean. This does make us know one another better because we have come into Christ's service together. Yes, I am glad, too."

They walked a little farther, saying nothing, then Laurel spoke again.

"I am going to try to grow in the spiritual life," she said thoughtfully. "Mrs. Gray has asked me to go to her evening Bible study class, and I am going. Will you have any place to go in camp that will help you to study the Bible?"

"I'm not sure. I'm afraid not. They do have services there that are not compulsory of course. I'll be looking around when I get back. That'll be my first concern.

Meantime, if you come on anything great, would you mind jotting it down and mailing it to me? I'd be interested, if it isn't too much trouble."

"I'll be delighted to do that," said Laurel. "That will be interesting, and also it will help me to remember what I have heard. I'll send you a résumé of the class every time. Of course if you get tired and bored and aren't interested any more, you can tell me so."

"I shall not get tired. I shall not lose my interest," said Pilgrim gravely. "I rather fancy I shall just live for those lessons to arrive. It will be great to have a link like that with you. And to feel that it is really through you that I have got to know God! If I had not come on you standing there alone in the road and needing help I might have gone right on not knowing or thinking any more about God or being saved than I ever did, and just as alone and hopeless as I have been through the years. You say I saved your life. Well, however that may be, you certainly saved my life and I shall be thankful to you throughout eternity. I'm saying this to you now because I'm going away, and I may never have another chance to *say* it to you. Of course I could write it, but this is the kind of thing that ought to be said if possible, not just written. It needs to be said in a tone that comes straight from the heart."

And then once more he stooped and touched his lips reverently to the tips of the fingers that he held warmly in his hand.

"Perhaps you think I am presuming," he said suddenly, "and I guess I am. If I were not going so soon, perhaps never to see you again, I would not force these things upon your notice. But you see I want you to know how I feel about it. I have to run the risk of your thinking me a fool, or that you think I am treating you lightly."

"I think it is *precious!*" said Laurel earnestly. "I shall always treasure the memory of what you have said, as the most beautiful thing that was ever said to me."

Her voice was very soft and husky and there were tears on her lashes. As Pilgrim looked down at her through the dusky moonlight sifting through the branches of the hemlock trees, she seemed to him the most beautiful girl he had ever seen.

"You see, I—*love* you!" he explained, his voice warm with feeling. "Oh, I know it is too soon to tell you a thing like that, and I cannot go on and say more as I would like to do, for I am a soldier, and I must go away tomorrow. There may never be any more time to tell you. And I wanted you to know it before I go away to face whatever God has for me to meet."

Suddenly Laurel turned and threw her arms about his neck, drawing his face down to hers and laid her warm lips full upon his with a quick tender kiss.

Just then the sound of footsteps came around the corner, only a few yards away, and Laurel wilted back into her place and went on very demurely.

"You rated that," she said shyly, "and you may take it with you to remember me by till you come again."

Pilgrim caught her hand and held it tight, steadying her to walk past the people who were coming. And then there were others, and still others, in the near distance. Church must be just out. A good many people were on the streets going home. So the two young people walked quietly along with no sign of their wildly beating hearts, or the joy that was all but overwhelming them. No talking at all till they came to the gate of the boarding house, and there was Mrs. Price standing in the front door talking to a woman, and keeping a sharp eye down the street.

"I'd better stop right here," whispered Pilgrim as he sighted the lookout. "It's just as well you shouldn't be questioned about uniforms you know."

"I know," said Laurel. "But oh, can't I see you again? Don't you know when you have to go? When is your train?"

"I think the last one leaves around four-thirty. If there's a chance at all I'll get in touch with you. Perhaps by phone. Do you know when your school hours close?"

"I think around three. But of course they may ask me to stay to get instructions for the week or something."

"Yes, of course. Well, we won't plan for anything. Just take what comes." He smiled sadly. "But—you'll be writing?"

"Yes, I'll be writing," said Laurel with a note of joy in her voice.

"You have the address I gave you?"

"Yes, safe and sound in my purse. But I have it in my memory too. Don't worry. And suppose you send me word when you arrive in camp please. I'll want to know if you got there all right you know, and if they are sending you away anywhere soon. Don't forget!"

"Sure! No, I won't forget!"

There was no opportunity for tender farewells now, for a bevy of young people were drifting down the street.

"Such a mob!" exclaimed Pilgrim under his breath, but he reached out and squeezed her hand again, and then with a mighty effort he tore himself away and hurried out of sight.

Laurel went on the few steps to the gate, went into the house and up the stairs, the landlady looking curiously after her and studying the way her hat was trimmed. It certainly was smart and becoming.

But Laurel hurried up the stairs, locked herself into her room, and went over to the moonlit window hoping to be able to catch a glimpse of Pilgrim. But he had disappeared into the tree-shadows. So she stood there for a little while looking out, her cheeks burning hot in the darkness at the memory of the kiss she had given him. Would he think her forward and bold? He evidently wasn't a man who went around kissing girls promiscuously. But oh how dear and wonderful he had been. And he had said "*I love you!*"

How the memory of those words thrilled her, even though they hid the possibility of war and death coming between them forever. But this was something that must not be thought of with sadness, just a great gladness that it was true. So queer and dear and true!

What would Cousin Carolyn say if she knew about it? Cousin Carolyn who wanted her to marry a rich, worldly man, a man who did not know the Lord Jesus Whom she and Phil Pilgrim had just taken for Saviour and Master. Oh, the world was wonderful all the way she had been led. Even though it brought sorrow and parting and hard days in the wake of every joy!

Two days, and then, *this!*

Then she went to kneel beside her bed and thank God that He had brought Phil Pilgrim into her life.

THAT first Monday at school was a day of excitement and hard work for Laurel. New things to learn, new pupils to meet, a whole day's program to put into practice, and with all this the necessity of doing it all as if she were accustomed to such routine, and were not just utterly new that day to the business of teaching.

But underneath it all there was a great gladness in her heart like a lovely tune that kept thrilling her. Phil Pilgrim had said "I love you" and again and again the words shot joyfully through her. Perhaps the sweet melody helped her to keep a poise through her unaccustomed duties, for more than one of her eager young pupils went home and reported, "She has the most Heavenly smile you ever saw! I like her a lot!"

As the day with its duties wore on, she found herself looking out as she passed the window, hoping against hope that she would see Pilgrim going by. Was he back yet from the work on Crimson Mountain, and would he have time to come by the school? Her heart was in a young tumult, wondering what time the school would set her free to go, and whether she could possibly meet him just to say good-by. She knew that he was hoping to sell his car this morning, and that he had errands at the bank and somebody's office. And he did not think it wise on her account to appear around the school house. But surely she would get away in time to get to the station to at least wave a good-by.

She was hindered a little when school was out, getting directions from the superintendent, talking with some of the teachers. After all this was her job, and she must not run away from it, much as she wanted one more glimpse of Pilgrim.

But at last she was free, and evading a group of teachers who would have lingered to talk with her she hurried to her car, and drove quickly to Mark's garage. And there stood Pilgrim's car, a stranger about to get in.

Mark eyed her with a familiar grin as she drove up.

"Has Mr. Pilgrim been here yet?" she asked.

"Yep. He just left for the station I think. He sold his car. Did you know?" and Mark nodded toward the old jalopy that was rolling away, almost sadly it seemed to Laurel.

"Oh, did he?" she said. "That's nice. He wanted to sell it."

"Sure he did. He wouldn't have no use fer a car down at camp."

"I suppose not," said Laurel pleasantly. "Well, I'll be seeing you when I want gas again, or repairs," and she drove on around a corner and headed toward the station.

It was very near to train time, and she hurried. She mustn't miss him now.

She saw him standing at the end of the platform, his baggage at his feet, looking out down the road. Was he looking for her?

Then almost at once he saw her and his face lighted. She drew up, parked a little way from the station and went across to stand with him. It was the end of the platform away from the town, and quite sheltered by shrubbery. How thoughtful he was, always protecting her from small annoyances that she had not even thought of herself!

And how good-looking he was, so tall, such strong fine features! How his brown hair waved away from his forehead where the army cap had made a crease. Then he was beside her looking down, and she felt again what beautiful eyes he had. Silly! She had seen them yesterday and noted it then, but he seemed now so much more interesting and desirable since he had told her he loved her. Going away! How terrible it was, and she had just found him! She must not surrender her thoughts to him so entirely. She was not a silly young girl.

But her glance met his, and her caution fled to the winds.

They talked a few minutes quietly. He told her what he had been doing on Crimson, how the work was finished, and he had arranged for care for his little cemetery. Mark's young brother was going to do that for him.

He asked her about her school, and she gave him a brief comical description of her day, her eyes dancing with just the joy of talking to him. And then they saw the train coming, and into both pairs of eyes there came a look of dread. Their time together was over! Only another three minutes perhaps.

There were a few people on the platform down nearer to the station where the train would probably stop. He measured the distance of the oncoming train, and then suddenly he stooped and gathered her in his arms for just an instant, holding her close, and kissing her with a caress that spoke many sweet messages.

"Good-by, dearest," he whispered. "Don't forget me. Be praying!"

"Oh, I will," she breathed softly.

Then he caught up his baggage and strode down the platform swinging onto the steps of the first car, and standing there as the train started, and passed her. She was smiling, tears on her face. His smile meaning so much as he saluted going by! He stood there on the step as long as the train was in sight, until it swept around the curve and passed on cityward, till he could no longer see the flutter of her handkerchief.

And if anyone had seen the new schoolteacher in the arms of a good-looking soldier boy, and looked curiously, trying to figure out who they were, the two did not know it, for they were taking snapshots in their hearts for use in the barren days ahead.

And so in due time Laurel got into her car, drove around awhile till she was sure she wouldn't weep, and then put her car in the garage at her boarding house, washed her face till the tearstains were no longer visible, and went down to a very poor Monday supper. Or maybe it was the tears that made it seem so poor. Or the stolid Byrger sitting across in that corner, boring her soul again with his gimlet eyes. Oh, she certainly must find a new boarding place!

But she was too tired to think about it tonight. Besides, she had other things to think about. She would go right to her room and be by herself.

But she found it was not so easy to be by herself. The stolid man with the gimlet eyes arose from his table just as she did and followed her out into the hall.

"Good evening," he said in his smooth insinuating voice, "we're fellow-boarders so I assume that makes us acquainted. My name is Byrger. Carl Byrger. What is yours?"

Laurel stiffened haughtily. She did not want to tell this man her name, but there was no point in being disagreeable.

"Sheridan," she said coldly. "Miss Sheridan."

"Glad to meet you, Miss Sheridan. How about a little walk this evening? I understand there are some pleasant views around this town. I'm on a new government project up on a mountain nearby. I thought we might walk up there and look the ground over. Would you like to go?"

"You'll have to excuse me," said Laurel severely, "I have work to do this evening."

"Oh, well, then tomorrow evening?" he said. His gimlet eyes had a mocking look in them.

"It's quite impossible *any* evening," said Laurel with finality. "My evenings are otherwise occupied," and she swept upstairs in a hurry. And then after she had locked her door she stood for a moment with her back against it, her hand on her heart, puffing as if she were out of breath, and her eyes blazing.

After a little she calmed down.

"Silly!" she said to herself. "I'm just silly. He's only a poor stupid ignoramus who thinks he can barge in anywhere and make friends. Maybe I was too hard on him. I could have been a little pleasanter about it. I could have smiled when I said no. Probably that's what a real Christian was meant to do. I don't need to accept his attentions of course, if that's what you call them, but I can be gracious about it. Maybe that's how you live up to your glory in your life, try to keep everything clean and fine about you so the glory can shine through. Well, I've got to study about that. Perhaps there's more to it than I've seen on the surface. Perhaps you have to get to the place where you find you can't do it of yourself. You've got to have Christ's help for it. I'll have to investigate."

Laurel calmed down at last and went over to her desk to examine the books she had brought home from school. It was most necessary that she go over the lessons she must teach the next day. The books were all new to her. So she settled down to work.

But she hadn't been at it more than a half hour when there came a knock at her door. She jumped up annoyed to be interrupted and found it was only the boy from the office saying someone wanted her on the telephone. Now what could that be? None of her intimates as yet knew where in Carrollton she was located, so it must be the principal of the school. Maybe some suggestion about tomorrow. Perhaps he hadn't liked the way she had done things today, and he was going to dismiss her. She half wished it were so, that she could get out of this town, and most of all out of this boarding place, at once. Only where could she go? Not to Cousin Carolyn's again. Not *ever!*

She hurried downstairs, annoyed to see Byrger sitting slumped in a big chair over in the corner behind the evening paper, quite near to the telephone, his gimlet eyes peering interestedly at her as she appeared. There! There it was again! She was in need of patience moment by moment, and she had none of her own. Would God supply it? It wasn't like polishing up a dirty engine room. Her own vigilance couldn't ever keep her spirit in leash. She must ask God about it.

She went to the telephone and spoke in a subdued tone, conscious all the time of the avid listener across the room.

And then suddenly her heart leaped up at the sound that came to her over the wire.

"Is that you, Laurel?" It was Pilgrim, and her voice broke into a lilt in spite of the listener.

"Oh—*yes!* Where *are* you?"

"I've reached camp. I promised to let you know."

"Oh, thank you! Thanks a lot!"

"Are you all right?" There was tenderness, and yet restraint in his voice, a voice that showed he knew there must be strangers about who might be able to hear him.

"Yes, I'm all right, and hard at work, getting ready for tomorrow. Did you have a pleasant trip? Oh, I'm so glad. And it was so nice of you to let me know that everything is all right. I—would have been worrying about it."

"Are you alone?"

"Oh no," said Laurel brightly. "There is always someone around. But they are very kind. They generally stop talking when anyone is telephoning. Of course it would be pleasant if they had a phone in each room, but if they did I don't imagine I'd be able to pay their price."

"Yes, I see. It's hard lines, but you always take everything like that cheerfully, don't you? By the way, around five-thirty tomorrow would you happen to be anywhere near Mark's?"

They were talking enigmas now, and both of them knew it, but just the sound of each other's voices was enough to satisfy.

"Why, I imagine so," answered Laurel almost gaily. "Yes, I think that would be possible."

"Okay. I might be able to give you an answer to one of your questions, you know."

"I see! Well, that will be satisfactory to me, I guess. Sorry we couldn't make it tonight though. It's always hard to have to wait."

"Yes, I know it," agreed Pilgrim. "I see what you mean, and I sympathize with you. I'm sorry I can't do anything about it tonight. If I were there I might be tempted to wring somebody's neck, but since I'm not, perhaps it's just as well for the other fellow. But, by the way, have you still got your glory?"

"Oh yes, indeed, I have. I wouldn't want to part with it, would you?"

"Not for all the kingdoms of this world. And say, doesn't it seem rather trivial to be considering the daily things of life when there are so much more important things going on? I hadn't thought of that before, had you, but I'm beginning to understand. It's probably best to let the matter take its course."

"Oh, yes, I'm sure!" agreed Laurel with a giggly laugh. "You're so amusing, you know. But, by the way, before you hang up, are you expecting to see Uncle Sam very soon? You *are?* How nice! And would you remember me to him? Give him my warmest love, please. He is such a dear! And I know he'll be glad I thought to send my love to him. He's always so appreciative!"

"You're not by any means kidding me?" said Pilgrim.

"Oh no, Mr. Stranger, I'm perfectly serious. If you can just get this order through before that Crimson Mountain affair gets done, it will make the biggest difference in this world."

"I'll see," said Pilgrim. "By all the signs it looks as if I might make it after all. Well, so long! and I hope to have better news for you tomorrow night."

"And say," said Laurel, "what did you say that number was that I should call if I need any special service?"

He mumbled a number and a word, and then, "Make it snappy! So long till tomorrow. And come alone if possible. We don't want any others in on this deal."

"Of course not," said Laurel indignantly, with an assumed grin. "Well, good night. I must get back to work. I'll be seeing you."

She hung up and vanished upstairs like a flash, not even looking toward the eager listener who had abandoned his newspaper and was watching her. It gave her great pleasure to turn her key in the lock so that the rattle of it was distinctly audible downstairs.

Then Laurel sat down and laughed, laughed till the tears came to her eyes, just to remember some of the silly things they had said to cover up the lilt in their voices. And then she pressed her fingers over her eyes squeezing the tears away, and smiled over the great thought that had been conveyed through all that covert language they had used. "I love you! I love you," every tone of his voice said it to her heart, and filled her with a deep sweet joy.

She had tried not to think too much about him all day, lest her heart would be too disappointed if he went away and forgot her. It hadn't seemed that he would be like that of course, that he would forget, but in spite of her at times she had been reasoning with herself, trying to show herself that she had trusted an utter stranger too much. That he might get among the other fellows and forget all about their wonderful meeting, and the flashes of wonder that had passed from eye to eye. But he hadn't forgotten, he *hadn't forgotten!* He had called, and he had understood that she was trying to tell him someone was listening. And now she had something to which to look forward tomorrow! Oh, it was not all hard and bleak, even if Phil Pilgrim had gone back to camp and she did not know yet what was coming next.

But down in the office the strange stolid man was sitting in the big chair staring off speculatively at nothing, trying to figure out what that telephone conversation might have meant. Was this beautiful girl possibly a spy or something, and had she been talking to a fifth columnist? Were they planning something that he must look into? It wasn't going to be a simple proposition to judge by the way she acted when he asked her to take a walk. She wasn't easy bait for a harmless flirtation. Perhaps she thought she had bigger quarry somewhere. He must take pains to find out who this girl was, and if possible what she was doing here. Here in this boarding house to which his mentor, Mr. Dexter, had ordered him to come. She had mentioned Crimson Mountain. What did that mean? Was she aware of what was going on? He must look into this.

To that end he sought out the landlady when a little later she came in from the dining room and went behind the desk.

"Mrs. Price, who is that very attractive young lady you have boarding here? I think she said her name was Sheridan. Where is she from and what is she doing here? She's not trying to get a job as stenographer, is she, because I'd like to get in on the ground floor on that proposition if she's in the running. She looks to me quite capable, and of course she's easy to look at."

The cunning look came into Mrs. Price's eyes.

"Oh, Miss Sheridan you mean! Yes, she's quite attractive. She's real aristocracy, she is. She used to live around here when her father was living. They were wealthy people and lived in one of the best houses in town. Yes, she certainly is smart, and she oughtta be. She's had advantages, she has. Her folks were real swells, and she went ta college herself, after her pa died. They tell me he lost most of his money before he was took, and I guess she ain't got so much now. Anyways she took a job. She's teaching in the high school. Ain't it awful the way changes come to the best of folks, and you can't tell from one day ta the next where you're gonta be hit! I always say it's best ta save when ya can. But then, most any bank can break. It's hard ta know what ta do. But she is an attractive girl. I don't blame ya fer admiring her."

"And you don't think she'd like ta be a secretary?"

"I don't know nothing about it," said the landlady.

"Does she understand shorthand and typing?"

"I don't know nothing about it, I tell ya," said Mrs. Price, "and I can't be bothered like this. Ef ya wantta know whyn'tya ast *her?* I got my work ta do."

Byrger went out a little later and walked around the block, taking in a good view of every side of the boarding house, and observing that there was a light in the window of the room that Miss Sheridan occupied, but the shade was drawn down tight. He could not even see if she was moving about the room. Then he stood for a long time at the gate looking off toward Crimson Mountain, and seeing in imagination the scene of his coming activities.

And up in her room Laurel was sitting at the crude little golden oak desk, writing a brief note to Phil Pilgrim.

Dear Philip:

I hope you understood my peculiar conversation this evening. The telephone is in the office, and the stupid-looking man with eyes like gimlets, who came in that car with the other two that night, was sitting only a few steps from me, listening with all his ears. You certainly were a good sport to understand the situation.

It was good to hear your voice so soon. Thank you for keeping your promise.

May our Heavenly Father guard you and keep you and give you comfort.

Your friend,
Laurel

BY Tuesday morning of that week trucks were rolling up Crimson Mountain carrying lumber and brick for the new munitions plant, and workmen were hurrying into town in response to announcements posted on highways and in newspapers, and special notices in many places. A great many came to Mrs. Price's boarding house to secure rooms and board, though many found the price there too high for the wages they were not yet receiving, or might not receive at all. Many went about the town searching for other abiding places, some of them making journeys to a nearby city and returning with trifling tents, in lieu of more permanent dwellings.

Thursday evening about eight o'clock there came another telephone call for Laurel, and the man Byrger was at his usual post, on watch again behind the evening paper. That paper made a convenient shelter for his watchful operations.

But it was not Phil Pilgrim's voice that answered Laurel this time when she gave her grave quiet "Hello!" It was nevertheless a voice which she knew.

"Hello! *Hello!* Laurel, is that you?" There was haughty reproach and annoyance in his voice.

"Yes, this is Miss Sheridan." Laurel's voice was cool and composed. There was no intimate recognition in it to give the listener a clue.

An offended laugh followed.

"Why the formality, Laurel? Don't you know me?"

"Why surely, Adrian. But it happens there are others in the room. I was only being a bit dignified. How are you? Oh yes, I'm quite well and very busy. I was sorry not to see you before I left, but it couldn't be helped. Circumstances spoiled my plans, and I didn't even succeed in calling you up as I promised. I did try once, quite early, but you weren't back yet they said. And I've been meaning to write a note of apology, but I've been so busy since I came that I just didn't have time. I was sure you would understand. But how in the world did you know where to call me?"

"Oh, I have ways of finding out when I want to very much," said Adrian loftily. "But what I called you for tonight is that I have something very special to show you, and I'm coming over there in my car around one o'clock tomorrow and get you. So please be ready. Just street clothes will do. We'll go somewhere for lunch and then I'm taking you to see something I am sure will please you immensely."

"Well, that's very nice of you, I'm sure," said Laurel, trying to speak interestedly, "but I couldn't possibly go anywhere tomorrow. I'm busy all day, every day except Saturday. I have a job you know."

"A *job!* But that's absurd! I'll soon finish that! Be ready please at one o'clock!"

"That's quite impossible!" said Laurel coldly, "and I don't *want* my job finished, thank you. I *like* it. I'm afraid you'll have to come when I say if you wish to see me."

"Well, this is the most ridiculous thing I ever heard of. *You* with a *job!* What do you think you are doing? Trying to get something back on your cousin for something that doesn't fit in with your strait-laced notions? Well, then, when *will* your highness come?"

"I tell you I have no day sooner than Saturday. If it's a mere drive somewhere, not too far away I'll be glad to go with you Saturday afternoon. I can be ready by one-thirty Saturday."

"I will call for you at ten o'clock Saturday morning!" said the haughty voice.

"Oh, very well," said Laurel coldly, "I can arrange to go in the morning instead."

She was speaking sweetly, with no sign of the annoyance she was feeling. She didn't want to go riding with Adrian Faber Saturday at any time. She would much prefer to visit Mrs. Gray and get information about the Bible class next week. But she had promised Adrian that she would call him up when she got back to the city after having failed him at his hunt club party, and she must be honorable and polite and make up for that breach of etiquette of course. Well, perhaps it was as well to get her position with regard to this young man thoroughly defined at once and not be annoyed by him all winter. She must make him understand once for all that she was a schoolteacher and could not dance attendance on him every time he chose to call her.

So she listened to his haughty reproval, and condescending palaver, sweetly, and let him talk. While the stolid face of Byrger watched her every move from under half-closed eyelids, and puzzled over that name "Adrian" that she had spoken. Could that by any means have been Adrian Faber to whom she was talking? But of course not, for that did not fit in with the rest of the picture. Or did it? Not as he had worked it out. It couldn't be possible that Faber was interested in a girl who appeared to be—well perhaps she wasn't. He would have to watch her. What time was that she promised to be ready to go somewhere with him? Saturday afternoon? He must make it a point to be where he could watch the house then. Could it be possible they were going up Crimson Mountain? Trying to pry into some government secrets? How much did that girl know, anyway? It certainly was queer he couldn't get anywhere with talking to her. She must be pretty keen.

But Laurel, all unaware of the espionage that was being set over herself, went annoyedly up to her room again. Adrian! Why did *he* have to come on the scene now? Oh *why!*

Then suddenly she began to think into her heart and see what was the matter. She was disappointed that the call had not been from Phil Pilgrim. In spite of the fact that she had been talking with him Tuesday night from Mark's garage, and he had told her that he would not be able to call her again that week as he was on duty at the hours when she was free, she had unreasonably hoped that she would hear his voice when she took down the receiver. And then suddenly she laughed at herself. What would Cousin Carolyn say if she knew that she was actually *preferring* a poor young soldier boy to the great Adrian Faber? *Disappointed* because she had to go with him on a ride, instead of with Phil Pilgrim!

Well, it was true.

And only last week she had actually asked herself whether she could ever bring herself to marry Adrian if he should ask her. Though she owned honestly to herself now that she never really had answered yes to her soul's query about it. Wasn't that plain enough when she actually went away that Saturday morning to think things over, not sure whether she was coming back for that wonderful party or not? Well, the question was answered for her now. She would never marry Adrian

Faber. She couldn't imagine any thrill coming to her if Adrian should tell her a thousand times that he loved her. In fact Adrian would not be likely to say those same words. He would put it in some more stilted language. Some less fervent sentence. He would say, "I'm really quite fond of you, my dolling, and I am convinced that you would make a marvelous hostess for my home. I could be proud of you, going anywhere. And I'm sure you would grace any situation where I might be placed."

Adrian was much too modern to call any emotion of his *love*.

Then she laughed again.

"Well, we'll just settle any plans like that, my lad," she remarked to the walls of her boarding house room. "I shall be too busy all winter to go on parties and expeditions, or spend week-ends anywhere with you." She would say it so firmly that he would see it was not of any use to keep at her. She would show that she was definitely out of the picture as far as he was concerned. And then of course he would likely drop her and forget her. Well, that didn't hurt her any.

Having settled this question definitely she went on with her study. She was actually getting interested in the study she was pursuing each day to get ready for her class, and looking forward with pleasure to being able to impart the knowledge she had gained to her pupils.

And then the thought came to her, suppose she had not met Phil Pilgrim that day on the mountain side. Would she perhaps, even now, have been considering whether she wanted to live a life with Adrian Faber? If she had never seen a man like Pilgrim would she have been satisfied with Faber?

And then her heart shrank back at the thought. No, oh no! Never satisfied with that!

Saturday morning was clear and bright. Laurel had

been hoping against hope that it would be raining, and she could therefore have an excuse to beg off from the drive. But the sun shone gorgeously, and old Crimson Mountain, still regal in her display of flame and gold, beamed down upon the little town at her feet as if she were doing them a favor to keep her gay robes on so long when the time of year had come that she might have put them off.

Laurel stood by her window and gazed on the rich display of color, thanking God for its beauty. She had not yet done anything about changing her boarding place, partly because of that wonderful view. She could not bear to miss a day of it. There might be other places in town from which you could see Crimson Mountain as well as from that window of hers, but she hadn't found any yet. And the young men who were purported to be desiring that room for the winter had not yet materialized, so she had let the matter ride. It wasn't yet a week since she came, not till Saturday night, and the Price woman had said nothing more to her, so she felt fairly safe about it. But anyway when she came back from that ride with Adrian she would spend Saturday afternoon looking up another possible place, so if her room was demanded she could get out in a hurry.

And then, just a little before ten o'clock the mail arrived and brought her a nice thick letter from Pilgrim's camp. She was glad she had gone downstairs because otherwise Byrger would have had the first handling of the mail. She had noticed that he was generally on hand when the postman came. But the mail had arrived unusually early this morning and she had the opportunity to find her own letter before he appeared on the scene. She slipped it quickly into her handbag and then went out to the front porch to await Adrian's coming.

He was not long in arriving. Byrger was still immersed in his own letters, sitting in the office in his favorite chair, poring over a closely written letter, not aware that Laurel was on the front porch.

So it was that he missed entirely seeing Faber's luxurious car drive up and take in the girl that he had resolved to watch carefully this morning.

Laurel hadn't even opened her letter yet, and it was annoying to see Adrian when she had been counting on a few minutes to herself to read it. But she put down the thought, tucked a handkerchief carefully about the letter, and snapped the clasp of her handbag sharply. That letter would be something to come back to when this ride was over. Better get it over as soon as possible.

So when she caught the flash of the distinguished looking car driving toward the house she hurried down the walk and was already at the gateway as it stopped.

Adrian's haughtiness relaxed. He was pleased that she had not kept him waiting.

"Well, you're ready bright and early," he said swinging open the car door and helping her in, before ever Mrs. Price could rush from the kitchen to see what car was stopping before her door, and before Carl Byrger was aware that his bird had flown.

"Didn't you bring an overnight bag?" questioned Faber. "Have you nothing with you but your coat?"

"That's all," said Laurel smiling. "I must be back early. I have a lot to do this afternoon."

"Yes?" drawled Faber as if he had inside information that didn't fit with that. "Well, we'll see, after you've seen what I have to show you. I think you will sing a different tune, little lady. However I suppose you can easily borrow what you need."

"Why, if I need anything, of course," said Laurel amusedly. "You never think I mean what I say, do you, Adrian? But I assure you I am quite changed, now that I'm a working woman. And if you have any such ideas as changing my plans and getting me back too late to carry them out, why you better take me back at once, for I'm telling you I can't *possibly* be late coming home."

"Oh, all right," said the young man in an evasive tone, "we won't talk about that yet," and he stepped on the gas and fairly flew over the road on a new route that was not at all familiar to Laurel.

"Why, where is this," she asked, looking about her. "I don't recall this road at all," as he veered directly away from the main highway that went through Carrollton. "It must be a new road. How pretty it is here."

"It *is* a new road," said Faber. "I thought you would like this. There is a view of the river a little farther on that is most picturesque. I was hoping you hadn't been here and I might have the first privilege of showing it to you."

"Why, I'm delighted to see it," said Laurel politely, wishing secretly that she might have had a chance to read just a few words of her letter before they had started. She did so want to know if Pilgrim was to be sent far away, soon. But she talked on about the lovely road, as they went mile after mile into a region of magnificent estates that she had never dreamed were in this vicinity. Lovely new houses built with curious architecture, beautiful grounds ablaze with autumn flowers, curving drives brought out by trees and shrubbery that were calculated to be a setting for seclusion and beauty. Now and then a club house and golf grounds that spoke of wealth and aristocracy. And as the way wound on, she wondered where she was being taken, until at last the car suddenly turned into a great stone driveway, and swept up to a building entirely hidden from the road, and most attractive in its appearance. Big stone arches curving about walls that seemed to belong to some castle of old.

"Oh," exclaimed Laurel, "how very lovely! Can this be a club house or—does some friend of yours live here?"

"No, no one lives here at present," said Adrian as they drew up to the door and the car stopped. "It is a new house, recently completed. I have had my eye on it for a long time. I have brought you here to see it. I want to know if you would like to live here?"

Laurel looked at the young man in amazement. Was he joking?

"Would *I*—like to *live* here? What in the world do you mean, Adrian? What an absurd question to ask me. Is it some kind of a joke?"

The young man gave her an annoyed look.

"No, I am not joking," he said haughtily, "I never was more in earnest in my life. I have an option on this house and I want to know if you like it. Do you?"

"Like it?" said Laurel, still more puzzled. "Why of course. It is a beautiful house. Anybody would like it, wouldn't they? It's a charming place. It's a mansion, a palace! But why should you need my word for it? Or were you only having it in mind to show me something very wonderful?"

Laurel's tone was mocking, her laughter gay and not at all self-conscious. Adrian looked at her with an annoyed frown again.

"Can't you be serious?" he said. "Do you, or do you not like this house? Would you like to live here?"

Laurel's face sobered.

"Why, yes, I can imagine that life under some circumstances could be very pleasant in such a house as that. But of course for practical purposes it would scarcely be fitting for *my* station in life."

Adrian looked at her merry dancing eyes and his indignation rose.

"You certainly are very trying, Laurel," he said severely. "I am endeavoring to discover whether you want me to buy that house or not? Can't you understand?"

"Whether I want you to buy that house or not? Why Adrian, I should suppose *you* were the one to be suited in a house you are thinking of buying, not me. I of course would have nothing to do with a matter like that. If you like it, and since you have money to pay for it, and to run it after you have paid for it, I should think it might be a very lovely idea for you to buy it."

Adrian gave her a withering glance.

"You're being quite obtuse, aren't you?" he said indignantly.

Then he swung open the door of the car.

"Get out," he ordered. "We're going inside."

"Oh, really?" said Laurel. "How nice! I'd love to see inside a house like that. But we mustn't stay there very long," she glanced at her watch. "It's getting late and time to start back. We've come a long way, you know, Adrian!"

He did not answer her. Just stalked up the steps and flung the door open wide, his eyes furious.

Laurel paused on the threshold and exclaimed at the beauty.

"Why, it's all furnished!" she exclaimed. "How marvelous. What a darling color scheme, and how it all fits together harmoniously! Oh, I'm so glad to have seen this lovely place!"

Adrian's tenseness relaxed.

"I was quite sure this would appeal to you," he said, almost offendedly.

"Well, it was nice of you to take the time and the trouble to bring me here!" said Laurel uneasily, realizing that there might be something more to come.

He led her into the great living room, that was so wide and high and deep that it was almost big enough to be a ball room, and seated her in a luxurious chair.

"Now," said Adrian, "I want to talk to you. You have been very difficult, and I did not expect to have to present this matter in such a state of mind, but since you have chosen to be this way I suppose there is nothing to be done about it but speak very plainly. I have bought this house and furnished it to the best of my ability, in an endeavor to please you, and to get ready a place where we could come after we are married and live a pleasant normal life. I have arranged that any article of furniture that you do not like can be returned and you can choose other articles in its place. I have brought you here today to show you what kind of a home, and what kind of a life I expect to give you, and I have arranged everything so that we can be married at once and begin living here. I dislike delays very much, and I felt that if everything was ready you could not put off the wedding long. Fortunately any purchases you wish for your own wardrobe can be made in a few hours, and I don't see why we could not be married at once. That is in a few days."

"Married!" said Laurel staring at him in amazement. *"Married?* Why, Adrian, I have no idea of marrying you! I could not marry you!"

"Indeed!" said Adrian. "And why not? Am I so objectionable that you cannot entertain that thought?"

"Why no, Adrian, you are not objectionable. You have always been most kind and nice to me. But I could not marry you."

"And why not?"

"Because I don't love you, Adrian." She said it solemnly and sweetly, and he stared at her with a look of one who didn't quite understand, but could not but admire. Then he turned with a haughty fling up of his chin, and a sneer on his lips.

"Oh, Heavens! Laurel, that's old stuff. Don't you know that love is outmoded long ago?"

"Sorry!" said Laurel with a lift of her own firm little chin. "It may be outmoded with some, but not with me." She said it definitely. "I could never marry anyone unless I loved him."

"Oh, that's nonsense, Laurel! Love comes after marriage, didn't you know that?"

"No," said Laurel. "I think that is one great reason of many divorces. So many people marry when they are not sure that they love each other. I think it would be unbearable to be married to one you didn't love with all your heart. Don't you?"

Adrian shrugged his shoulders with a calm smile.

"There is always divorce," he said. "One doesn't need to feel that the matter is too final."

"Adrian! Do you mean that?" she asked.

"Why certainly I do," said the young man, regarding her amusedly. "Don't you? You have to if you want to keep up with the times."

"But I don't, Adrian. There is sin in the times. More than there has been for generations. And that matter of divorce is a part of it. Even if I loved you, Adrian, I would *never* marry a man who believed that 'there is always divorce.' In fact, Adrian, even if I loved you I couldn't marry you, because you and I do not think alike on hardly any subject. We could never live together and be happy."

"Oh, now that's absurd, Laurel. Don't you know that it is generally accepted by everybody that when people live together they get to thinking alike? Before a year of married life was over for us *you* would begin to think as I do. Those things adjust themselves, you know."

"And you think, Adrian, that before a year, *you* would have begun to think just as *I* do?" laughed Laurel. "You wouldn't believe in drinking, nor gambling? You wouldn't delight in night clubs and Sunday house-parties, and all those matters on which we have never agreed? You think that *you* would come to think as *I* do? Is that what you are trying to say?"

"Heavens, no! I didn't say that. I said that *you* would come to think as *I* do. You know when there is a difference of opinion between husbands and wives the final word is always the prerogative of the husband, for man is the head of the house and has the deciding right."

"Yes," said Laurel. "*That* would be the way that it would be! That is what I am sure it would be. That would mean that a marriage like that would take away my right to think for myself. And that is why I could never marry you! No, Adrian, it wouldn't be possible, even if we loved one another. And I *know* that we do *not!*"

"What makes you think that?" asked the man. "Do you know what love is?"

"Yes, I think I do, Adrian. And I think that in the relationship of a man and a woman it is the only thing worth while."

"Oh!" he said with a sneer. "Do you think that that could make up for poverty and hard labor, and pain, and a lack of all the good things that go to make life in this world worth while?"

"Yes," said Laurel looking at him steadily, "I do. I know people who have been through all that, and have been happy in spite of it, because they have loved. It seems to me that without deep love marriage would be a travesty. And I do *not* love you!"

He looked at her steadily, emotions flitting over his handsome facile face like angry clouds trembling over the pleasant blue of a summer sky. There was disgust, fury, scorn, intolerance, determination, and then lofty amusement.

Suddenly Faber arose.

"Forget it," he said in his drawling amused tone. "Let's go look at the house. I certainly am not coming all the way out here without a chance to show you the whole place."

It was a part of his regular tactics, this sudden change of attack. It always took his victim off guard, and for the time won him a count.

Laurel gave him a frightened puzzled glance and then rose from the comfortable chair. Instantly he was by her side, assisting her to rise, leading her through the lofty rooms, throwing open doors that revealed lovely vistas, giving a glimpse of fragile glass and priceless china, breathtaking in its beauty. And there still remained in the girl's consciousness a memory of values that made her know how costly all this display was that he was showing her.

Faber seemed to know by instinct just what would most appeal to this girl he had brought here to tempt her from standards that seemed so firmly fixed in her soul. He was watching her now each step as they progressed. Through the library with its costly volumes in rank after rank of tooled leather bindings, gold lettered. The exquisite bits of statuary here and there in nooks just made for them, the few magnificent paintings that seemed like glimpses of the real world. Up the stairs so broad and low with luring views from arched windows over mountains lovely in their autumn garb. He could read her enjoyment of it all in her beautiful young face, and it was as he had planned. She reflected beauty as if she were a glass.

But there was something missing. Some quality of utter surrender to the things of the senses, that he had not counted on. What was it? What had happened to her since he had last seen her? It was as if she had become immune to the things of his world. She could see its beauty, but it no longer had power to move her as it used to. What could it be that had changed her? It did not seem possible that in so short a time, a few days, something should have so influenced her that the things he had counted upon could no longer draw, had lost their power. It must mean that something greater than he knew had gained an influence over her.

And then he set his worldly mind to work to discover what it could be. Some other man of course, he decided. Who was it? Some hick-lover she used to know in her school days. It must be that, for surely nothing else could lure her back to that dead-and-alive little village in the edge of the mountains. No power less than an old lover could make her willing to pass up a fortune and take up with being a schoolteacher. And now what was he to do?

She must see everything in the house of course, while she was here, and he made sure of that, until Laurel was fairly tired out. He devoted himself to her in a charming way until he almost made her believe she had misjudged his harshness and worldliness.

And yet she could not but remember the gentleness and care of another young man who had walked beside her a few days ago. If she wanted to she could not admire this man with that other in her mind.

She looked at her watch as they were coming down the stairs at last from a survey of the upper stories and the amazing wealth of luxuries that had been flung at her feet.

"But, Adrian," she exclaimed, "look what time it is. I must get back. I told you I had things to do today."

"Yes," said Adrian calmly. "We're getting back all in due time. First we're taking lunch at the country club nearby, and then we'll talk about going back."

In troubled silence she succumbed. She had promised to go to Mrs. Gray's and she didn't like the idea of disappointing her, but she must handle this matter in a manner that would not bring her trouble later. She must show Adrian that she was in earnest. She must finish the matter once for all.

But Adrian said nothing more about marrying until

they had finished lunch. Laurel had tried to be as pleasant as possible, so that he would have nothing to blame her for.

And at last, when he saw her begin to gather up her things and put on her gloves, Adrian spoke, as if he had never left off the one topic that had been in their minds all the time.

"Laurel," he said, "you've changed. What's happened to you?"

"Changed?" said Laurel. "Yes, perhaps I have." She looked at him thoughtfully. "Yes, something *has* happened to me. I didn't think it showed on me—not yet!"

He studied her again, almost alarmed now. She was going to admit it. That looked sort of hopeless.

"What is it, Laurel?"

She was still a minute and then she looked up with a sudden blaze of light in her face.

"Why, I've accepted the Lord Jesus Christ as my Saviour, and it's changed a lot of things in me. It's made things clear in my mind that have been sort of muddled for a long time."

He looked down at her for a moment with amazed disgust, and then he said with a new kind of contempt in his voice:

"You don't mean you've turned religious on me, do you? *Good night!* Is it as bad as that? Well, I only know one thing. You ought to see a psychiatrist at once before this thing sets in and gets a strangle hold on you. You don't want to lose your mind, do you?"

Laurel smiled.

"Oh, there's no danger of that," she said almost eagerly. "I was never so happy in my life. I'm sorry for you because I can see you don't understand, but perhaps some day you will, and now, Adrian, please take me back. I really must go at once. I'm going to be late for something I had planned to do."

"Do you actually mean that you *want* to leave this house and go back to that terrible boarding house where I found you?" His eyes were so utterly unbelieving that she had to laugh.

"Oh, that boarding house is rather terrible I know," she admitted. "I mean to get a better place as soon as I have time to look around. And your gorgeous house is marvelous. It isn't that I don't *like* it. But it is not for me. It is not where I belong, and I must go back to my work and to the place God has shown me He would like to have me stay for the present at least."

Adrian scarcely spoke all the way back, and he drove like an express train, with a stern disapproving look on his handsome face. Somehow it did not depress Laurel as it might have done, for she was thinking of other things, and preparing a pleasant little speech of thanks for him when he would be leaving her.

But Adrian was planning how he would go straight to Cousin Carolyn and beseech her to get Laurel to a psychiatrist as soon as possible before this thing went any farther.

THERE was a light on Laurel's face during that drive home that Adrian couldn't understand. He watched her furtively a good part of the time, and tried to think what caused it. She didn't seem depressed as he felt she should since she had turned fanatic. She seemed really happy, and her eyes were glad eyes.

As they approached the town of Carrollton and Laurel caught the light of the setting sun on Crimson Mountain something flared in her face like sudden joy as if she really loved that town, and Adrian asked her suddenly:

"Who lives in this town that makes you so fond of it?"

She turned with a bright smile.

"Oh, there's no one much here that I really know," she said, "a few old friends of my mother's. And the old home is here where I was brought up. I'm teaching in the same school I attended as a child. It's rather interesting. But there's nothing in the town itself to draw me of course. There are pleasant memories, otherwise any other town of this size and style might have been as pleasant a background for my first job."

"Well, then I cannot understand it," said the young man in his most displeased tone of voice. "There certainly must be something behind all this. I cannot think that just a sudden spurt of religion is responsible for what you have done, turning away from my offer of a happy and luxurious life. You certainly must have lost your head over something."

"No," said Laurel, suddenly sober. "I haven't lost my head. I have just come back to the things my mother and father taught me. And please, Adrian, don't think me unappreciative of the honor you have done me in asking me to marry you. I *do* understand what it means, and I *am* grateful to you for the lovely day you planned for me, the marvelous house you offer me as a home, and the unapproachable position you offer me in the world. You have been most kind and pleasant to me since I have known you. I am only sorry to have to disappoint you for the reasons I have tried to make plain to you. I do not love you in the way a woman should love the man she is to marry, and I do not feel that we could ever agree in our ways of looking at life. I would never be willing to give up what I feel is right, and you would never be willing to acknowledge that there is such a thing as right and wrong in this world. Now, please understand that this is final, and let us not have to talk about it any more. Let us be friends and not enemies, please. And I thank you for the pleasant day."

He had stopped the car by the roadside. He looked down at her, and was still a long time, studying her. At last he said in a stern cold voice:

"Very well, we'll talk no more about this. But I want you to understand that I am *not* giving up! I *mean* to *marry* you. I can wait, and I expect to see you change your mind when you get over this fit of fanaticism. But just to humor you in what seems to be your chief objection to me, that you think I do not love you, I will tell you that I am actually very fond of you. And that I am looking forward to growing more and more fond of you as the years go by."

Laurel's chin was lifted in a quick challenging motion.

"I am sorry that you take that attitude," she said gently. "I am sure I shall not feel differently. I have been looking into my own heart and life, and I am seeing things very clearly. I have nothing but friendliness for you, but I know that your standards and mine are utterly at variance, and I have no desire to be at war with my conscience from this time forth, not even if I were to gain the whole world as represented by that lovely home which you have been showing me today. And now, will you please drive me to my boarding place?"

In utter silence, with an almost stony face, he drove her to the ugly house where she was staying, and helped her to get out. Then he lifted his hat, said a cold good-by, got into his car and sped away. Just once he turned back and looked at that big ugly shabby house, with the girl he wanted mounting the steps. It was unbelievable that her devotion to *any*thing could make her choose a life at that Carrollton boarding house, to a life in the suburban mansion he had been showing her. It was incredible! She must be crazy! And yet, her eyes were clear. She looked perfectly calm and sane! Poor kid! She was in earnest. Well, perhaps a psychiatrist could bring things out straight for her. He must go and see her Cousin Carolyn tonight and see if she couldn't do something about it. He didn't intend to give that girl up. Even in her stubbornness she had been most charming, had more appeal than any girl he knew. Her eyes were so very blue, and if she could just get rid of those fanatical ideas of hers she would be a peach.

So he drove away, past gorgeous old Crimson Mountain and never even noticed it.

But about that time Carl Byrger was climbing Crimson Mountain in company with two rough looking fellows, newly arrived, who had been domiciled in the third floor back of Mrs. Price's boarding house, and then been told off to be shown some strategic points of the place where they had come to labor. Their names were Gratz and Schmidt.

Laurel went flying up the stairs. At last, at last she could read her letter!

She locked her door, flung her hat and coat on the bed, sat down by the window, pulled out her letter and read:

> Dear Laurel:
>
> Now that I am so far away from you it fills me with a sense of great daring to be calling you by that lovely name, so intimately. It seems that somehow I must have dreamed all our sweet converse together and am presuming, to go on daring to claim a right to address you in this way. It seems as if it cannot be true that I have ever dared to hold your dear hand, or touch your lips with mine, or tell you that I love you. A thing so wonderful cannot really have happened to me. I must be dreaming still.

Suddenly Laurel put her head down and brushed away the two happy tears that had jumped out upon her unawares, before she could go on reading.

It was a very precious letter, all too short. She read it over and over again, thrilling anew at the sweet memories of those precious hours when he was with her, thrilling at the thought that those memories were staying with him also.

Then suddenly she remembered her engagement with

Mrs. Gray, for which she was already late, and jumping up she began hastily to get ready, her face still glorified with her joy over the letter.

As she turned her car toward Mrs. Gray's she was thinking of her letter, and scraps of it ran through her mind, each phrase a delight. She had never known it would be like this when she would come to love someone.

Then it came to her that Adrian could never inspire in her the joy and delight that this stranger man had brought. Not with all his wealth and station. How different her day would have been if it had been Pilgrim who had taken her to see a house he had prepared for her!

She almost felt a pang of pity for Adrian Faber. He had tried to plan a pleasant time. He had seemed to care. And yet, even his attempt to offer a line of affection, had not rung true, "I am actually very fond of you." Ah! How different that was from "I love you."

Then another sobering thought came to her.

He had asked her who was in that town that made her want to stay there. Well, there was no one here, but Phil Pilgrim had *been* here. It was her experience with him that had made her know with entire surety what love could be, and had helped her to clarify matters in her own mind and to know beyond the shadow of a doubt that she did *not* love Adrian Faber. But this was not anything she could have told Adrian. His case had to be dealt with alone. If Adrian were the only man on the earth who admired her she would not want to marry him. And it was no fault of Phil Pilgrim's that she felt so. It was simply that in Phil Pilgrim she had seen what a man could be, and she could never accept anything less than that for herself.

"Now, forget it!" she ordered herself as she drew up at Mrs. Gray's door. "I have told Adrian I could not love him, why do I have to worry about it any more? I will ask my new Lord Jesus to settle this thing for me in the right way. He can protect me against plans and schemes of those who want to order my life for me."

Adrian had said he was going to Cousin Carolyn and talk about a psychiatrist. Well, Cousin Carolyn might come down to see her and make things unpleasant for her of course, but she had no real authority over her, and could do absolutely nothing. She was of age now, and her own mistress. She must not be afraid of Cousin Carolyn. She had a Lord who would protect her, and she would stay where she was, and not yield to their persistence. She would not go riding or walking or partying or anywhere else with Adrian Faber again, no matter what excuses he made to get her consent!

Then she walked into Mrs. Gray's house smiling, and hugging to her heart the thought of Phil Pilgrim's letter.

"Oh, my dear! I'm so glad you've come. I had almost given you up!" exclaimed Mrs. Gray.

"I'm so sorry!" said Laurel. "I had promised to do something this morning, and had no idea it was going to take me so long. I'm afraid I've hindered you a lot. Perhaps you wanted to go somewhere. If you did won't you let me take you there now?"

"Oh, no, child! I didn't want to go anywhere. I was just disappointed to lose the time with you. And now to make up I'm going to keep you all the evening and we'll have a real time together. Unless of course you have some other engagement for evening. Of course I must remember that I'm an old woman and you're a young one, and I mustn't barge in on your engagements."

"Please don't feel that way," smiled the girl. "I would rather be with you this evening than anywhere I could go, and I'm going to enjoy you a lot as a friend if you'll let me."

"Let you? Of course I will," said the little lady, drawing up a rocking chair beside a table where an open Bible lay across a big concordance. "Now, suppose you tell me what it was you wanted to know about the Bible. What has been troubling you?"

"Oh, there is so much I don't know where to begin," sighed Laurel.

"Well, you should have a regular Bible course," smiled the lady, "but since you are teaching and probably have a pretty stiff course to get acquainted with at present I suppose that won't be possible for you to arrange just now. But I would suggest that you join our Tuesday night class. You can't have a better teacher. He comes down from the city every Tuesday and returns that night, and he is connected with the big Bible Institute there. It's marvelous that we are able to get him."

"Oh, where does the class meet?"

"Right here in my house, my dear. We felt a good many might come to a class in a private home who would not come to our chapel because it is undenominational, and some of them have been made to feel that that is a wicked thing. So for the present we are meeting in these two rooms. Now, shall we get to work? Would you like me to run over the work we have had in our class so far this fall?"

"I certainly would," said Laurel.

"Well, that's nice," said Mrs. Gray. "I only wish Phil Pilgrim were nearby and could run in and study with us."

"Yes," said Laurel, her cheeks getting pink, "wouldn't that be nice!"

Then they settled down to work.

Laurel was fascinated with the lesson as Mrs. Gray made it plain to her, and when they finally put aside their study and went out to the pretty kitchen to get ready the nice supper that had been preparing in the oven while they worked, Laurel thought what a pleasant home this was and what a dear friend she had found.

"This is going to be wonderfully interesting to me," she said eagerly as they sat down to the little round table with its appetizing meal. "And here's a question that has come to me several times since we were here last Sunday. Tell me, what happens if we fall away from the Lord, after we have accepted Him? Does that disqualify one from salvation?"

"My dear, *no!* A soul that is once saved is *saved*. The Lord never lets go His own. We can have perfect assurance of that. 'He that heareth my word, and *believeth* on Him that sent Me, *hath* everlasting life, and *shall not* come into judgment, but *is passed* from death unto life.' Those are Jesus' own words."

Laurel's eyes opened wide.

"Judgment!" she said. "Do you mean we don't have to come to judgment? But I always supposed that everybody had to be at the judgment and give account of all the sins they have committed while they lived."

"No, dear. No judgment for your sins, because they have already come to judgment in Jesus' death. If you have accepted Christ as your Saviour then your sins were judged in Him as He took your punishment for you on the cross. There is a judgment later when rewards are given for the way we have lived the Christian life after we were saved, but it has nothing to do with being saved. It is *not* a judgment of sin."

"Why, Mrs. Gray, that is wonderful! I wonder if many people know that."

"Yes, they ought to. People who study their Bibles should."

"Then if we sin after we are saved, it doesn't undo what Christ did for us?"

"No, dear. Of course we still have that old sinful nature and will have while we live on this earth, but Christ died for our sin. His death covered *all* our sin, past, present and future. All the sin you did commit, all the sin you are committing today, and all the sin you will commit. He took it all upon Himself. You'll find a great deal about that in the sixth of Romans. We'll look at it after supper."

Laurel looked amazed and puzzled.

"It is wonderful," said Laurel. "I never knew there were deep things like that in the Bible. Answers to all the questions and troubles that come to us."

They had a delightful evening, going into this and that question, as Laurel came up against new things that she had never understood.

She went home rather late, put her car in the garage, slipped in the side door and up to her room without meeting anyone, for which she was glad. But when she unlocked her door and stepped into her room shutting the door silently, she heard voices just outside her window, on the upper porch, where usually no one went.

Carl Byrger, and the new men, Armand Gratz and Godfrey Schmidt, had come back to the house a little before the bell rang for the evening meal, and were given places in the far dining room. Mrs. Price always did her best to seat her boarders with regard to social position. The front dining room was pretty well filled up with what she considered "the elite." Laurel Sheridan was obviously in the most desirable seat in the front dining room.

But Laurel Sheridan of course was not at dinner that night, and did not see any of the new people who had come to the house while she was gone.

Gratz and Schmidt were neither of them troubled by self-effacement or shyness. They considered that anything in the house was theirs by rights. Weren't they paying their board like anybody else? So they had no sooner mounted to their small third-story room after dinner, than they slowly drifted about the third floor taking in all its few points, trying all the doors, opening one that was not locked, just to find out if there were better rooms than the one that had been assigned to them. They examined the articles left in the unlocked room, then went back to their own room, looked out the window and discovered the uncovered porch down below them. They decided that would be a good place to sit, so they put on sweaters and descended the stairs. After mulling about a bit they found the door to the porch, and marching in took possession of the three rickety chairs that had been out there all summer. It was just about the time that Laurel walked into her room and shut her door.

"Hey! Look out!" said Schmidt. "What was that noise I hear? Some door shut? What?"

"Nuthin' to worry about," said Gratz.

"But, these rooms are all occupied the woman said. Careful how you speak."

Then Byrger, hearing them step out on the porch, appeared at the door.

"Oh, here you are. What you saying? Anybody hear you? Na, you don't need to worry. This middle room won't be occupied till tomorrow. Two fellas from the city coming, Winter and Rainey. And the room up at the end, some dame has that. But she ain't here. She's been away mostly all day. Probably won't come back till late tomorra. I think she has friends where she stays weekends."

"Oh, that's good!" said Schmidt. "Then you sit down, Byrger. I gotta question. Where we gonta get the dynamite when we get ready to give 'em the works?"

"Oh, there'll be plenty of that around. We'll swipe some now and again, when they don't keep such good count of them. Times when there are a lot of men working on blasting and things."

"So!" said Gratz thoughtfully, "and where'll we keep 'em till the time comes, so we can get 'em quick?"

"I know," said Schmidt. "I saw two gravestones up the other side of the road this afternoon. We can make a place behind those stones. People won't expect dynamite in a graveyard. Some folks are superstitious. They don't like dead folks. They're afraid of ghosts!"

"That's an idea, Schmidt," said Byrger, "keep that in mind and be ready to work it when you see a chance. I guess you boys'll make a go of it all right. But don't mention it to the two men that are coming tomorrow. They think they know it all! Especially Winter. He thinks he's the boss. It's just as well for you to keep your secrets to yourselves, at least for the present."

"Okay!" agreed Schmidt, and then after a pause, "You know who b'longs to those gravestones? Anybody who can make trouble if they find out?"

"No, I don't think so. I heard it was the man who sold the government the land for the plant. He won't likely be around. I heard he had went away. But you gotta hide that stuff so well nobody can't find it but yerselves anyway, ya know. And you gotta get it out in the dark. You gotta fix it so's you can find it in the blackest dark. You can't run no risks when the time comes."

"Okay!"

Then Gratz spoke.

"When ya gonta pull this job off?"

"Well, not for sometime yet. You'll have plenty time to make yer plans and get ready. The plant ain't built yet. It's goin' up fast, but there'll be some time fer ya ta work at laborin', an' throw off suspicion. You gotta act awful dumb ya know, so nobody won't suspect afterwards. Soon's they get the plant built then I begin my work. Those two other fellas will be helpin' me, but I'm the inventor, see? They're not supposed ta know the secret. Ner *you* don't know neither, see? They're supposed ta hev bought this invention from some great man out in a perfessors' college, an' he sent me here to put it up for him. I hadta study with him for a long time till he could trust me to put the thing in shape, and after it's supposed to be ready to work and produce, he's liable ta come here any time he likes and keep check on it whether it's doing the work right. Somebody on the other side heard about this secret and had me sent over ta get in on it. That's how I got it. And there wouldn't be any way to hold up the production of it, unless something was ta blow it up, just as they was ready to produce. See? That's where *you* come in."

From their first word Laurel had sat breathless in the dark on the foot of her bed, just as she had dropped down when she first heard them discussing whether she was in her room. If she could hear their voices as clearly as that, then they could hear her every movement. It was at first mere self-preservation that kept her quiet. She thought they would not likely stay here long and then she would be rid of them. But when she heard the word dynamite she held her breath in fright. What was she listening to? Were these men planning something dreadful, some gangster's job, or some terrible disaster? She had read of fifth columnists. Was this something like that? Or were they merely discussing some difficult work they had to do about building the plant? Oh, she wished she knew. Of course she was utterly ignorant on such subjects. It might be that all this talk was perfectly legitimate and she just did not understand it. But it sounded very tricky and crooked.

And then suddenly she sat up very straight and caught her breath again as they spoke of those two white stones by the roadside as a possible place for stowing dynamite. Her head whirled at the thought. She thought of the roses she had herself laid below those white stones, and the sacred little service in the sunset that she and

Phil Pilgrim had held together. It seemed that they were almost blasphemous, speaking of those two graves in connection with their evil devices.

Then as they went on and Byrger outlined the whole wicked scheme, her heart was beating wildly. Oh what was this, and why had it been revealed in her hearing? Had she some responsibility about it, as if a plot to kill someone had been revealed, and she was the only one who knew about it? Surely someone else ought to be told. Who could she tell?

Not Mrs. Gray. She was only a woman. She would scarcely be likely to know about things like this. Not any of her father's and mother's old friends, even if they were at home. They would simply think she was in a terrible place and ought to be rescued from it. Well, perhaps she was. But that was a secondary consideration. This was something that ought to be attended to *at once*,—yet what could she do? To whom could she go who would know what to do? Not the young minister in Mrs. Gray's church. He was away at his seminary all the week, and anyway she did not know him well enough. This was a serious matter. It would take someone with courage and wisdom to deal with this. She must not trust just anyone with what she had heard. Not Mark at the garage, he was only an ignorant man, and would perhaps be afraid to meddle in such matters.

Well, she was afraid too. Who could help her? If only Phil Pilgrim were here he would know what to do! He was in the army and there might be some officer there that he knew who could work the matter out, but maybe that would be dangerous for Phil. Oh! What should she do?

Her eyes were wide with terror, and her breath came in quick little soft gasps. She must not make a noise. They must not hear her.

Gradually as she grew calmer and could think more

connectedly it came to her that there was no immediate danger. Nothing terrible would happen tonight. That stolid Byrger had said they must wait till the plant was finished, and this secret-something that was being made to figure greatly in the defense project of the country was completed. All that could not be done in a day. Even the dynamite that was to be hidden in those quiet graves was not here yet. There was nothing immediate that was going to happen. There was time to think it out and understand it. But if she only had someone she could trust, who would take over this awful burden that had suddenly been thrust upon her as a duty, and carry it, and bring it all out right, how good it would be!

It was just then it came to her. The memory that she did have some One to whom she could bring her burden.

"Casting all your cares upon Him, for He careth for you." Just a little verse from out her childhood, and she bowed her head and prayed in her heart:

"Oh God, I am weak and frightened and ignorant. I don't know anything about this, and I don't know how to do anything about it. Won't You please take over for me, and work this thing out the way You want it to be, so that the secret that is so necessary to safety here in our country shall not be lost, and that lives shall not be sacrificed. If there is anything You want me to do about this, please show me what it is, and help me to be wise about it, and not afraid. Help me to know that You are carrying on. For Christ's sake I ask it."

And just then she heard Byrger say to the men, "Well, come on, fellas, time to hit the hay! Besides it's getting chilly out here. Come on, let's go in." And then she could hear their heavy shoes squeaking down the hall and up the stairs. Byrger went inside his room and shut the door. Finally she knew they all must be asleep. But she stole around her room quietly in the dark, for if any of them were about she did not want them to know she had been in the house, and might have heard them. And so at last she lay down to rest, her head pillowed on prayer.

IT was a bright beautiful morning when she awoke. The crimson and gold from the mountain shimmered off in the distance like a flame in the sky. Though somehow she felt it was fading, and must be near its end. The leaves were beginning to fall. The winter was almost here. The wind was cold as she shut her window and went about her preparations for the day.

Then she remembered what she had heard last night, and a great depression settled over her. No, she must not take that burden upon herself again. She had given it to the Lord, and she would leave it there!

But she was glad that Mrs. Gray had asked her to come and spend the day and go to church with her. Well, she wouldn't go down to breakfast this morning. She had a box of crackers in her room and a few grapes. Those would do in place of breakfast. She did not want to meet those awful men who had talked that way last night. She was sure her telltale eyes would let them see that she had heard them, and until she knew what she ought to do about it she wanted no contact with them. Perhaps she ought to leave this boarding house at once.

Or, could it be possible that she had a duty to stay here and perhaps get more information, and help to avert some kind of a calamity? And what was that they had said about Tom Rainey and Bruce Winter? That they were coming here? Would either of them be ones she could tell? No! She did not altogether trust either of them. Oh, she didn't want to see them now.

She ate her crackers and grapes, and bided her time till she saw the three men who had been on the porch last night, go out of the house and take their way up the mountain road. Then when they were out of sight she slipped out of the side door, got her car and was soon away.

But all day long, though she had a happy time with Mrs. Gray, she had the matter of the munitions plant in her mind, as though she were a soldier under orders, awaiting a command. She had a feeling that while the Lord had taken the burden from her, He yet would be expecting her to do something when He got ready to tell her what it was. How she was to know she had no definite idea, but she felt she would understand when the time came. Till then she could only wait.

Several times during the day she was on the verge of telling Mrs. Gray, yet again and again she hesitated.

When she went home that night, she looked up at old Crimson and thought of what might happen up there some night, when Carrollton was asleep. How there might be an explosion that would shake the mountain, and then a fire that would light up the sky for miles around. Old Crimson on fire! And if that ever happened some night while she had been sleeping, and she should awake and see that crimson glow she would never forgive herself for not having told somebody. And yet who could she tell but God, who would have any authority to do anything about it, or who would know what to do?

That night Rainey and Winter arrived late, and grumbled noisily in the hall over the fact that there was but one room for the two of them.

"I told you, Mrs. Price, that we wanted two rooms. We were to have the end room and this next room that you have given us."

"Yes, but the man you brought with you took the end room. He said he was the head of your bunch of men anyway and he had the right to choose."

"The *head!"* sneered Winter. "He certainly is *not! I'm* in charge of this bunch, and I intend to have that room!"

"Well, what'll I do with Mr. Byrger? He won't like it. He's very hard to please."

"Put him in that other room, up by the front stairs. Or else, perhaps *I'll* take that. Let me see it."

"No sir, you can't see it tanight. The young lady is in that."

"Young lady? I thought you told me you didn't know if she was going to stay."

"Well, I wasn't rightly sure then, but she's staying. I haven't asked her yet if she means to stay all winter. I wouldn't want ta lose her."

"Well, would you rather lose all three of us?" glared Winter. "I'm in charge of this gang I tell you, and I want them together. We have to have conferences sometimes about the work you know."

"Well, I'll ast her in the mornin' if you insist," said Mrs. Price, "but I can't promise you nothin' till then. Anyhow ta night you'll havta take that middle room. It's all I got vacant at present, except a little one in the third story where an old lady is leaving tamorra morning. I could ast her ef she would mind sleepin' with me tanight ef that would suit ya, and one of you could sleep up there."

The two young men cast a withering stubborn glance at each other, and then Winter answered crustily:

"No thanks. We'll camp together tonight, but tomorrow morning we want separate rooms on this floor, or we leave and go somewhere else."

Then Laurel heard the two go grumbling to their room, and she lay there quietly trying to think it out. Certainly she did not wish to stay here any longer. Just how should she manage it?

Tomorrow morning was Monday and she must be at school on time. That was her limitation. Therefore she must be up early in the morning. She must pack her things as quickly as possible for moving, and she would not go down to breakfast. She did not want to meet these young men, not at present anyway.

Both Tom Rainey and Bruce Winter had called upon her several times while she was with Cousin Carolyn. They had taken her to a couple of parties and out to dinner, and if she met them now it would probably involve her in all sorts of complications. They might become as troublesome as Adrian Faber. Meeting them later, just casually, it would not be so hard to deal with them. But meeting them at a common abiding place was another thing.

So she packed early next morning and had all in readiness to move, watching the window meanwhile until she saw the two young men get into their car, and drive away. Then she rang for the house boy and told him to take her baggage down to her car. She went ahead of him and opened the garage door, and the back of her car, and when everything was stowed carefully inside, just as when she had arrived, she drove her car around to the front of the house and came into the office.

By this time Mrs. Price had arrived at the desk, two red spots glowing on her high cheek bones.

"What's up, I'd likta know?" she demanded stormily. "What'rya tryin' to do? Sneak away on me?"

"Oh, no, Mrs. Price," said Laurel pleasantly. "You

see I happened to overhear the disturbance in the hall last night, and that your two boarders who wanted my room had returned, so I thought it would be a good thing for me to get right out so you wouldn't lose any rent."

"Well, really, Miss Sheridan! What kind of a thing is that for you to do! I didn't ast ya ta leave. You shouldda come and ast me whether it was all right for ya ta stay. You was sa anxious ta keep that room, so I put them two men together. Ef they don't like it they can lump it. Now you just call that house boy and make him take them things o' yours right back upstairs! I'll make it right with them two men."

"I'm sorry, Mrs. Price. I'm afraid I can't do that. I've already arranged to go to a friend for awhile, and I don't think I care to come back here. I understand Mrs. Frisbie on the third floor is leaving this morning, and you know it isn't so pleasant for a girl to be rather alone in a house full of men?"

"What's the matter with the men?" snapped Mrs. Price. "They're all good respectable men, ain't they?"

"Why, I guess so," said Laurel. "I wouldn't really know. The ones I've met at all have been quite pleasant, but I think I would rather go where there are more ladies. I think I agreed to give up my room if your two boarders came, so I'm paying you for the week's board that is due, and I hope you will have a very successful season. Good-by! I'll probably see you again sometime. I must hurry to my school now."

Laurel gave Mrs. Price a cool little smile and hurried away before that angry woman could think of anything else to say.

Laurel was grateful that she had a friend in Mrs. Gray to fall back on now. Mrs. Gray had often asked her to come and stay with her for awhile. She wouldn't *stay* there of course, but it was nice to feel that she could go there now for a few days and be confident that she would be received with a warm welcome. Of course it couldn't be permanent as Mrs. Gray expected her sister and her husband to visit her soon, and anyway Laurel felt it was better for her to be just a friend who could run in when she liked, rather than to settle down there permanently even if she were asked. But now she turned her car toward the school. There would not be time for her to go to Mrs. Gray's before school.

But when she got to school she found a note on her desk that the janitor said a lady had left for her.

Surprised she opened it quickly, and read:

> Dear Laurel:
>
> I've just had a telegram from a dear friend up in the country who has been taken very sick. She wants me to come to her at once. I shall have to leave immediately. Will you do me the favor of telephoning the class that they will meet Tuesday night at Mrs. Bristol's house, 1728 Maple Road? And will you also please ask Mr. Stanton to meet our teacher's train and take him to Mrs. Bristol's?
>
> I am sorry to make you all this trouble, dear, but I don't know who else I could ask who would be able to do it. I am enclosing the telephone list and I hope you will excuse me for being so hasty. I must make the next bus.
>
> Thanking you,
> With a great deal of love,
> Rosalie Gray

Laurel sank into her seat in dismay. Now what was she to do? It would not be hard work to call up the class and give them the proper message, but what was she to do herself?

Then she heard the gong sounding for the opening of school, and the students came marching through the halls and turning into their various class rooms. Her own entered just then and took their places at their desks and in a moment more the usual morning procedure began like clockwork. She had no time to think about her own problems, though occasionally the matter would come to her mind like a thorn in the flesh reminding of its presence.

At morning recess time Laurel drew a small piece of paper toward her, while one of the other teachers was trying to explain how disagreeable old Miss Fenton had been to her when she told her that her niece would have to go back to the lower grade because she wouldn't study and couldn't keep up with her class. And when the other teacher had gone on to tell somebody else her troubles, Laurel looked at the paper and found she had written:

POSSIBILITIES
Tea Room ?
Hotel ?
Y.W.C.A. (Is there one?)

And what could she add to that meagre list? Should she go to the principal and ask questions? Were there other boarding houses in the neighborhood? Somebody would know. Yet she shrank from putting her predicament before any of the teachers. They would one and all set to work to turn heaven and earth for her. Insist on her coming home with them. And she didn't want to do it. She wanted to be independent.

Now what was she going to do? She didn't want to ask anyone in the school about a boarding place, because there were some foolish girls who were so crazy over her that they would demand that their parents take her in to board, and that might be very embarrassing. No, she had got to work this thing out by herself.

All the morning as she went through her daily schedule she was trying to think the problem through. Oh, if Phil Pilgrim were only here he would find a right place for her. Ah, but she had God! She must put the matter all in his hands. Rest it there.

So she prayed for guidance.

At noon Laurel went to the telephone and called up the tearoom, asking if they had any vacant rooms, but again she found the tearoom vacancies were all filled. She asked if they knew any other places where there were rooms, and was given a couple of addresses that might be possibilities.

"There are so many new workers at the munitions plant you know, that I'm afraid you'll find it hard to locate any vacancies," said the proprietress of the tearoom helpfully.

She glanced at her poor little list, and telephoned the hotel. Yes, they had a few rooms, fourth floor, no elevator. She got into her car and drove slowly by the hotel, but was not impressed by the company who lolled about the piazza. Pilgrim had told her it was no place for her to go.

She went to the post office and asked about a Y.W.C.A. but was told there wasn't any. Then on the way back she eyed several tourist places, but somehow none of them appealed to her. What was she going to do? Was she too particular? Surely there must be some other boarding house that would be fairly cheap and comfortable.

At her desk during a study period after lunch time she wrote a brief letter to Phil Pilgrim, realizing that his letters must no longer go to Mrs. Price's house.

Dear Phil:

This is just a hasty note to ask you to address any mail you may be sending to General Delivery till further notice. I am clearing out from my boarding place this afternoon and am not just sure yet where I am going. Will let you know the definite address as soon as I am sure that it is all right.

The other place got too full of workmen for the new plant, and the women all left but one so I thought I'd get out also. Those two acquaintances of mine were among the new arrivals, so I thought I'd better go before I had to meet them. Thus the haste.

The school work is going strong and I like it.

When do you have to move, and where? I wish you were here. I'd like to ask your advice about something.

Yours as ever,
Laurel

This she would mail when school was out, and then she would go out and find some place to stay that night. If worst came to worst she would go and ask Mark's advice. That was an idea. Why not?

So she got through her afternoon work calmly, excused herself from the attentions of her admiring pupils, and a teacher who wanted to talk, and got out on her job.

She mailed her letter and then started on a slow drive around the streets that would be most convenient to her work in case she found a boarding place.

There were plenty of cozy little homes, but none to which she quite felt like applying. They seemed like private houses. They had no signs out for either boarders or lodgers. And then all at once she saw a meek drab little figure walking along a side street, with a familiar slump to her shoulders, and a familiar droop to her head. Was that Mrs. Frisbie? Perhaps she would know of a place.

So she drove up to her and called: "Mrs. Frisbie! Is that you? I wonder if you can help me. You've left the boarding house, haven't you? So have I."

"Oh," said the quiet woman lifting those very sad eyes of hers admiringly to the girl. "Yes, I've left. She doubled my board and I couldn't afford it any longer. I wouldn't have stayed that long if it hadn't been cheaper than anywhere I knew then. What's the matter? Did she raise your board too?"

"No," laughed Laurel, "but some men came into the hall opposite my door last night and raised a terrible rumpus because they couldn't have my room. They wanted two rooms together. And when I heard you had left I decided that it was a men's boarding house and I'd better find some place where there were more women. But it seems it isn't so easy to do that, now that munitions plant is here."

"No," said Mrs. Frisbie, "I guess not. Everybody's taking in boarders, and the men are arriving fast now. I understand there's to be a hundred more come in this afternoon to work on that plant. They're trying to get it in shape to produce as soon as possible. And you haven't any place to go? Why, that's too bad. I should think the school might look after you somehow. There'll be somebody glad to get you. But that doesn't look after you tonight, does it? Well, yes, I do know of one room in the house where I am, but it's not a fancy place. Everything is very plain and homely, and they're plain people. They're good as gold, but they're not your class of people."

"Oh, my dear!" said Laurel aghast. "Please, *please* don't think I'm high hat. I'm only too grateful to know of a respectable place, and I am sure anything that is good enough for you is good enough for me. At least for a few days till I can make sure I have found the most convenient place for me. Where is it, Mrs. Frisbie? Is it near here?"

"Why, it's about three blocks away. You turn up that corner—" the shabby gray glove pointed ahead.

"Were you on your way there, Mrs. Frisbie?"

"Why, yes. I came home early from my work today to get my room in order."

"Well, won't you get in and ride with me?"

"Oh, thank you!" Mrs. Frisbie climbed in to the welcoming door that Laurel swung open. "That's kind of you. I was a little tired. I got up pretty early this morning to get my things out for the grocery boy to take for me. I didn't have so many, but I couldn't carry them all and Mrs. Price said if I didn't get them out by eight o'clock she'd have to charge me for another week."

"The old skinflint!" said Laurel indignantly. "Well, Mrs. Frisbie, I guess you and I are in the same boat. I wouldn't be at all surprised if she sent a lawyer around to see me to demand board for the whole winter."

She laughed lightly as she started her car, and Mrs. Frisbie relaxed her shy anxious face into an almost merry crinkle.

It was a bald old brick house standing stark and alone in a wide scrubby lot before which they presently drew up. A dilapidated barn hovered in the offing. There wasn't a tree on the place, and only a huddle of dirty withered leaves in the corners of the gaunt chimney that soared above the roof, to show that autumn was swirling around in the neighborhood. The tired old window shutters had once been green, but now they were faded to a sickly bluish nondescript color that did deadly things to the dull old red of the bricks. Some of the slats were out, giving the appearance of a blind dog with a bandage around one eye. One shutter was off its hinges lying on the ground, another with but one hinge sagged dismally, and still another had vanished entirely, but those were on the off side of the house and Laurel did not see them. The old front piazza had lost some of its underpinning and drooped unstably. There was a distinct hole in the tread of one of the front steps. The sickly woodbine that some brave householder had tried to train, had lost every leaf, and the knobby pale stem on which they once grew clung with a frail tendril to a crevice in the chimney, waving forlornly back and forth in the wind. It wasn't a cheerful looking place, and Laurel's heart sank as she took it in with a single glance.

But it was getting dusky already, and she did not know where else to go, so she got out of the car and went in with Mrs. Frisbie.

As she stood on the dilapidated steps she turned and caught a glimpse in the dying light of old Crimson Mountain. Ah! She would not entirely miss that sight if she came here! It made her feel somewhat at home. Then the door opened and there stood Nannie Gilbert, one of her own scholars, and she caught her breath. Nannie, a shy sweet girl, with plain ugly dresses, and never any of the trinkets and adornments that other girls seem to manage no matter how poor. Her hair, straight and black and bobbed in an old-fashioned way, was unbecomingly held back by a black ribbon tied around her head; a ribbon that never seemed quite adequate for its duty, and was continually letting down one straight lock in her right eye. Nannie Gilbert! So this was her background! No wonder she looked like that! Poor Nannie Gilbert!

Nannie smiled shyly.

"Why, it's Miss Sheridan!" she gasped softly. "It's wonderful to see you here! Come in, won't you? But—there isn't any nice place to take you!" She stopped short in the hall and glanced toward a door at the right which was closed, then went on. "You see—mother's fixing the parlor—into another room—to rent."

Her voice broke and seemed almost to fade away, but Laurel smiled and patted her shoulder. "Oh, that's all right, Nannie. I don't need to sit down. I just want to see your mother for a minute. Is she here?

"Yes, she's here. I'll call her," and she vanished inside the door at the end of the hall, whence Mrs. Frisbie had also disappeared.

Laurel found herself standing alone in a big empty hall whose floor was covered with badly worn oilcloth quite frayed at the edges, and she smothered a desire to giggle. This was such a funny place, and such a funny thing to happen to her! She turned about and looked out the open door. There before her in the light of a great red ball of fire stood Crimson Mountain, facing her clearly, with a halo of the last golden trees across its forehead. Dear old Crimson Mountain. Ah! She was not alone!

Then she heard steps coming and Mrs. Frisbie returned with a shy, tired-looking woman behind her.

"Miss Sheridan, this is Mrs. Gilbert," she said. "I told her you wanted to see if she had a room for the night, and perhaps longer if you didn't find the place you wanted near to the school."

Mrs. Gilbert studied her, and then slowly her face lighted up as she met Laurel's smile.

"Sheridan!" she said. "Then you must be Nannie's teacher?"

"Yes," said Laurel cordially. "But I didn't know Nannie lived here when I came with Mrs. Frisbie. I'm very glad to know you. Nannie is a very sweet girl, and she works hard in school and is a great comfort. I'm very proud of her as a scholar."

"Well, she's just crazy about you," said the shy

mother blushing. "I'd be proud to have you in one of my rooms, only we're not fixed up very fine. We haven't got any very grand rooms. There's a room in here. It was our parlor, but we're thinking of making it over into a bedroom. It isn't rightly done yet, but you can see it."

Mrs. Gilbert flung open the closed door by her side, and there stood the room, stark and almost empty, just a couple of chairs, a golden oak desk, an old-fashioned four poster bed, the head board and foot board standing up against the wall, the mattress and springs lying down on the floor. Over in one corner there was a high shelf with a row of hooks under it, and a calico curtain tacked half across the front. An evident plan for a clothes closet.

The dismay in Laurel's face must have shown as she turned toward Mrs. Gilbert, still smiling bravely.

"Oh! Is this—have you any other—?"

"Yes, we have one other room. It's up the stair. It ain't very big but it's close to the bathroom. Come right this way and I'll show you. Nannie, run see if that stew is burning and turn the gas a little lower till I get back," Mrs. Gilbert stood aside and let her honored guest climb the stairs ahead of her.

It wasn't a very large room they led her to. Just the end of the wide hall partitioned off, a curtained corner closet, a cot, and a shelf in the other corner with a looking glass over it for a dressing table. Laurel had never seen such make-shifts for furniture. There was besides a small rocker with a cushion made of a dark patchwork quilt. The whole thing touched her tremendously.

Then she turned and there was Crimson Mountain looking down at her more intimately than she had seen it yet. It was picked out sharply like an etching, against a sky that had in these few minutes put on a clear veil of pale green, with little flecks of clouds, varitinted, softly edged with light. And in this light the building which had been going on during those hectic days stood out clearly, showing its progress, showing the outlines, the rough stone work, the brick walls, the piles of lumber, and the crude board scaffold. Then, as a rent came in a deeply purple cloud, the sun, a dying ball of ruby like a jagged drop of blood, shot out and gave that fiery look to sky and mountain and the air about, then slowly, slowly dropped down behind old Crimson and was gone! Almost at once the dark came down and seemed to wrap about the mountain, like a hand wrapping up a precious package.

Laurel turned back sharply to the waiting Gilberts as they stood gazing breathlessly, watching her. What did she think of their poor attempts at grandeur? Would she take it?

But Laurel was struggling with a great emotion. The mountain had spoken to her and it was her mountain. Hers and Phil Pilgrim's—and God's.

"Yes," she said with a huskiness in her voice, "I'll take it. Yes, this one please! I like the view! I'm not sure for how long, but I'll take it tonight, and we'll talk about the rest tomorrow night, shall we?" She finished with her pleasant smile that made them all her abject slaves. "And now I'll go down and get my things," she said.

Suddenly from the shadows behind her a figure developed.

"Yes, ma'am. I'll go down and help you," said Sam Gilbert, Laurel's young scapegrace of a scholar who could always provide an alibi for any difficulty which he got tied up with. He accompanied her downstairs and out to her car, proudly walking ahead and waiting for her instructions when he reached the sidewalk.

So Laurel's luggage was transferred from her car to the second-story hall bedroom. Laurel, turning back, carrying as many small articles as she could manage, and surrendering some of them to Nannie who came down the walk to meet her, suddenly wondered why she had said she would stay in this forlorn looking house. It would never have attracted her if the day had been fresh and she had been rested. But it was just that evening vision of the mountain that had decided her. She knew it now. Well, she didn't have to *stay* here but one night if she didn't want to. But if she had been hunting the town over for a place where Rainey and Winter would not be likely to find her she could not have found a better place. They would never dream of her being in a place like this. Still, if Mrs. Frisbie said it was respectable, why might it not be all right? The house certainly looked clean inside, dismal as the outside had looked.

Laurel disposed her garments, a few of them, under the calico curtain, got out the books she would need this evening, and her writing materials, and made herself ready for supper, which she had been told would be at six o'clock sharp.

And that supper came graciously up the stairs about ten minutes before six, in long appetizing whiffs of browned gravy and onions, with a pleasant addition of baking apples and cinnamon. Laurel was hungry. Perhaps the supper would not be so bad. The meal was an interesting experience to the girl, who had never known much about hard-working poverty.

The table was long and wide and a little bit rickety. As she sat down, she had the place of honor beside Mrs. Frisbie at Mrs. Gilbert's right. There were small coarse clean napkins folded in triangles, and a bunch of wizened marigolds in a glass in the center of the long table. Two generous plates of bread flanked the two ends of the table, and the main dish of the evening was the delicious looking stew, which had not burned, and had a most appetizing odor. It was brought to the table in an enormous platter and put in front of Mr. Gilbert, the bright yellow of its carrots, the white of its onions and potatoes, and the brown of its gravy making a pleasant blending of color.

The dishes were cheap ironstone china, and the silver plated and badly worn down to base in some cases. The knife and fork and spoon that Laurel had were fairly bright and newer than the rest.

Mr. Gilbert and the four men who worked with him, either on the farm or at the plant, came in with very clean hands, wet hair neatly combed, and unaccustomedly wearing coats.

Laurel had never seen a meal like this, but somehow it intrigued her. So this was the background of those two young people to whom she would never have come close enough to understand if she had not come here!

There were two small brothers younger than Sam, and a little girl. The children took the plates when the main part of the meal was concluded and brought in heaping plates of hot cinnamon buns and the baked apples with pitchers of cream. It wasn't an elaborate meal, but it was well balanced, and satisfying, and Laurel drew back her chair feeling that she had enjoyed that supper more than any meal she had eaten at Mrs. Price's boarding house. Moreover she was intensely thankful to be away from that house, and not subject to constantly meeting those two young men she had known in the city.

After supper Mrs. Frisbie and Laurel had a little talk together. Just a comparing of notes about Mrs. Price, a word or two about the new plant and what changes it would bring to Carrollton. Then Mrs. Frisbie spoke of her daughter away at college, and of the general state of things in the world, expressing the opinion that there was no hope or no help anywhere as far as she could see, and that for her part life looked pretty dreary.

So Laurel told her about the Bible study class that she

was attending, and invited her to go with her to the next class. To her surprise Mrs. Frisbie accepted with alacrity, and she was surprised at the sense of pleasure it gave her to have passed on the invitation and to find it eagerly accepted. It came to her that it would be nice to help bring another troubled soul into the joy of knowing the Bible. And mightn't it be possible also to get Mrs. Gilbert to go to the class sometime?

Thinking of these things her excitement over the talk to which she had been an unwilling listener Saturday night passed somewhat out of her thoughts, and the importance of doing something about it did not seem nearly so insistent as it had at first. Perhaps it was all nonsense, anyway, her idea that it was of importance. And yet again and again would come the thought of those two quiet graves. Dynamite! She must tell Phil Pilgrim, though perhaps it might only distress him, and make him feel that he must have the caskets moved at once. Well, perhaps he should. But she would wait till she had word from him again, for there was no telling where he might be by this time. He had seemed to think he was to be sent away almost at once when he last wrote.

So she lay down to rest on the hard narrow little cot in the front hall bedroom, and found herself thankful for having found at least a temporary abiding place. Mrs. Gray would be home in a few days and then perhaps she would ask her advice.

So she went to sleep with Old Crimson looking down toward her and the night lights around the new half-finished plant shining in her window.

MRS. Gray did not come back to her home for three weeks. Not till her sick friend was well again, and up, and able to go about her home as usual. But she wrote to Laurel, and Laurel wrote to her and carried on the business of the class for her in her absence.

A letter had come from Phil Pilgrim, mailed on a train, en route to a southern camp where his division was being sent for more intensive training, and to pass through more selective separation. Phil wrote that an officer had questioned him most carefully about his earlier training, and the line he had expected to take up. And when he had found that Pilgrim was interested in mechanical things, and had also had several responsible positions in managing men, he took down the facts, and told him there was a possibility that some men would be taken out of the class of privates and put where their training and inclinations would tell for the most in the war.

The conclusion was that he was more uncertain than ever where he was to be sent, or what his status was to be. He still had the feeling that his destination was out of the country somewhere. But he said that was only a "hunch" and it might not mean a thing. He expressed his entire willingness to go wherever God wanted him to be, and said that his experience those few days with her, and especially the night when they had taken the Lord for their Saviour, had helped him to accept gladly whatever was ahead. If he had one wish above another, it was of course, that he might finally be placed where he could sometimes see her. If that time ever came he would feel that Heaven had come down to earth.

It was a nice letter, but somehow it gave her a desolate sense of his being gone, perhaps forever. Now he would be in a new place with new interests and there was no hope of his getting off for a furlough when he was so far away. Presently he would forget all about their days together, and gradually he would stop writing. That was the way those things usually worked out of course. So when she had read it through a couple of times she sat down in her room and had a good cry. Then she remembered that they both had a Lord, and He would keep them, and perhaps some day they would meet again, in Heaven anyway, and that they would remember each other.

And of course if he forgot, she would likely forget too, though it didn't seem that that could possibly be, *ever!* Well, at least she had the memory of those days and an ideal of love between man and woman that she had not thought could be possible. She was glad for that. And she had a knowledge of the Lord that she had not had before. They both had that, and they had a pledge to pray for one another. So at least they could meet before God.

She washed away her tears and set about trying to find some way that she could help those dear Gilbert people. They were sweet people, even if they were crude.

She hadn't any idea of staying very long in that forlorn house, in that cramped up little room, and she didn't exactly like the idea of taking the big parlor, right down amongst the family. So she told them she would stay there for the week at least, until she had time to look for a place nearer the school. Then she interested herself in studying Nannie and Sam, and the shy, scary, capable little mother.

The second day she asked Nannie to ride with her to school, and on the way they picked up Sam standing on the corner and looking wistful. "Oh, gee! Ride in that swell car! Oh *boy! Sure* he would."

So they arrived at school in state, happy and silent, and the envy of all the other pupils.

"How come?" asked an arrogant senior of Sam.

"She's stoppin' at our house fer a few days," explained Sam loftily, and went on his way. When the word went around the scholars looked amazed, raised their eyebrows and said "How come?" again. Some expressed the belief to one another that the teacher wouldn't stay at Gilberts' long. She didn't look the style for that old brick house.

That afternoon Sam cleared out a wide place in the old barn for Laurel's car, and offered to put it in for her. He also got a new padlock for the barn and gave her the key. He was doing his best to pay for their rides to school.

Laurel smiled at them both, and then next day, discovering that Mrs. Frisbie's store where she worked was not far from the school, she invited her to go with them mornings.

So there began to be a pleasant little camaraderie between the four of them. Though the young people never said very much on the way, just sat still looking shyly important.

When Sunday came Laurel asked them if they would

like to go to a little chapel with her on the other side of town, and they scurried around in a lively manner to get their Sunday work done so they could go, their mother only too eager to make it possible for them.

"We ain't had much time yet ta think about goin' ta church," she explained, with a grateful smile on her face. "I'd like fer the children to go to Sunday School, but I haven't been able to manage it yet, and they haven't got very nice clothes to go to these big churches around here. Mebbe you wouldn't like to take them either, they not looking very dressy."

"Oh, my dear!" said Laurel, "they always look nice. And the people in this chapel where I go are not stylish people. They will look all right."

So the two young people went to Mrs. Gray's little church and sat and listened in wonder to a simple gospel, the like of which they had never heard before, for they had not been interested in the Sunday Schools that their mother had sent them to before, and had got out of going as much as they could. But this was different and they took to it with eagerness.

Mrs. Frisbie, too, got interested, first in the Tuesday night Bible class, and then in the chapel, and by the time Mrs. Gray returned was counting herself a regular member. Laurel was proud of her achievements in getting them to come, and Mrs. Gray was delighted.

"But, my dear, we must find you a suitable boarding place now," said Mrs. Gray. "I presume you are not very comfortable at a crude place like that. If I only had a little more room I would love so to have you here, but I find my sister and her husband are planning on spending most of the winter with me, so that crowds out that idea. But I think we can find you some place near by."

"Well, that's kind of you but, Mrs. Gray, somehow I feel I ought to stay where I am, a little longer at least. I'm getting a sort of hold on those two children, and they were leading such starved lives I want to show them the way to find the Lord if I can. And their mother, too. Mrs. Gray, she just lives in that dreary kitchen, making nice things for us to eat. They are very simple plain things but they are good. Things like fried mush and bread pudding. I never dreamed they could taste as good as they do, and she is so shy and sweet. I wish you would let me take you over there to see her sometime. I know you would like her, and she would be so happy to see you. She's another starved life. And then there are the three little children. I tell them Bible stories Sunday afternoons and you ought to see how they enjoy it. I thought maybe I'd coax them to your Sunday School."

Mrs. Gray looked at the girl with a tender glance.

"My dear, you are growing, aren't you? Growing in the knowledge of what the Lord wants you to do. You know, to witness for Him is the only thing we Christians are supposed to do down here, and I surely think you are witnessing. I'm so glad that Mrs. Frisbie is interested in the Bible classes too. She has a nice face and I must get to know her. But, my dear, isn't it very desolate for you over in that forlorn brick house? There doesn't seem to be anything beautiful about it, and you are one who loves beautiful things so much! There isn't a thing that you can really enjoy."

"Oh yes," said Laurel eagerly, "I still have my mountain. I wouldn't want to go anywhere away from that. It is such a wonderful mountain, and it fairly speaks to me, mornings and evenings. Even now that the leaves are falling, and the branches are so many of them bare, it has a sort of suitable look for the time of year, like an older person whose hair is turning sweetly white or gray. And you ought to see the sun and moon go down behind its top. A ball of fire, or a golden disk! I love to watch them sink."

"My dear, you are a poet! But that mountain will presently be spoiled by factories and chimneys, won't it?"

"It's rather interesting, even that, and the trees hide it mostly. You see I know that mountain pretty well, some parts of it. I've had some pleasant times up there. When I was a little girl there was a picnic up there once that was grand! And just this fall I've been up twice with Phil Pilgrim. You know he used to live there."

"Yes. I know. Do you ever hear from him now?"

Mrs. Gray flashed a quick look at the girl, and noticed the soft flush that crept up on her cheeks as she spoke of Pilgrim.

Laurel's eyes brightened.

"Now and then," she said nonchalantly. "He's just been sent to another camp, down in Alabama. He's not sure what that means. It's a sort of a place where they select different men to go into things they are fitted for. But Phil thinks he is probably to be sent abroad, or maybe to Jamaica, or somewhere away from this region. But he says he is still happy in the fact that he is saved, and still grateful to you for what you did for us both that Sunday you asked us to spend the day with you. I think he is real. I don't believe he will forget, nor grow away from the Lord. I think it meant a great deal to him."

"Yes," said Mrs. Gray, "I believe he really meant it. He is that kind of a boy. He does things in a real way. I used to think so when he was a mere child and used to bring me eggs and berries. He was so manly and business-like. I have enjoyed watching him grow up. Though of course I never had much opportunity to study him. I imagine he had a rather sad childhood."

"Yes," said Laurel, "he did. And he's done wonders in spite of it, from all I hear."

"Yes," said Mrs. Gray. "He was famous in college for

both athletics and scholarship. I often used to see his name in the paper. Do you know if he will be coming back here on furlough soon?"

Mrs. Gray was watching Laurel covertly, and noting the instant sad droop to her lips.

"I'm afraid not," said the girl. "He had a very decided feeling when he went away that he might never come back. He seems to think he is to be sent abroad. I don't know why. I think perhaps some officer suggested that he should apply for something in the line of his recent studies, but he didn't say what. I have an idea it was something that had to do with engineering. He didn't say much about it."

"Well, I'm sorry he had to go away. I was hoping he would be around here occasionally this winter."

"Yes, so was I," said Laurel, with a quickly suppressed sigh. "But I'm glad he knows the Lord."

"Oh yes!" said the older woman. Then the subject was changed and not mentioned again that day, but Mrs. Gray had a very good idea that those two young people were most congenial.

"This war!" she said to herself. "What terrible things it is doing to young people today!"

Sam was getting very intimate with his teacher, talking quite readily now, bringing out all the news he learned on his paper route, and in his goings here and there. And Nannie was beginning to study her teacher's garments, and the way she arranged her hair, and doing her best to torture her straight locks into natural looking waves, until Laurel took pity on her and showed her how to shampoo her hair, and put it up in curlers, and then to arrange it simply and softly about her face so that it would be becoming. The child had no idea how to make herself not only tidy but attractive.

Sam came in to dinner one night and announced excitedly:

"They been having a time up to the plant taday. They arrested two men and got two more under suspicion."

The men looked up sharply and frowned at Sam, and Laurel looked up startled.

"What happened?" she asked. "Why did they arrest them?" It was the first time she had realized that the plant was in shape for any of the troubles that had been plotted that night when she had been listening. Perhaps she ought to have written Pilgrim about it before. She had so hoped he would be coming back before he went so far away, or at least before he went farther. But she hadn't had a letter for several days and she was afraid he had gone.

Her eyes were on Sam. He forgot about the assembled family who were always critical when he tried to talk, and went on with his story.

"Why, ya see, they been missin' dynamite. Whole lots of it. At first it was only a stick or two, and they thought they had miscounted I guess or something like that, and then there was more and more gone, and they tried to check on the men, and at last they thought they had 'em. There's a guy up there named Winter. It was his business ta keep tabs on that dynamite, and he found how it was disappearing and he began ta watch, and now he's caught some, and he thinks he's got some others."

"Who did they arrest, Sam?" asked Laurel. "Did you happen to hear their names? Was it anybody from the village?"

"No, they were all foreigners I guess. At least the two arrested ones were. A coupla guys came here from somewhere across the water a little while ago. They claim they was born here, but this Winter says not. The names were Gratz and Schmidt. They don't sound like very American names."

Suddenly Sam's father spoke.

"Sam, who told you all that stuff?"

"Why it was Joseph Wilmer told me when we were walking down to the newspaper office to get our papers this morning. You know his route is next to mine and we often go together."

"How would Joseph Wilmer know anything about what happened at the plant last night?"

"Why, his father works up at the plant, dad, and he's on the night shift ya know. He told Joe this morning just before I met him."

"Well, Sam, you haven't any business to repeat things you hear like that. This is war times you know and it's important to keep these things quiet," said his father. "Now while there's so much talk about fifth columnists people ought to keep their mouths shut. You can't tell who's an enemy and will report things, and you can't tell what's important to the enemy. Just *you don't repeat* these things any more, see? And if Joseph Wilmer tries to tell you anything more that happened at the plant you tell him you don't want to listen to him. His dad ought to know better than to tell such things out where his kids will hear, and I don't want my son repeating them. Do you *hear,* Sam? That's a *command.*"

"Yessir," said Sam, subsiding into his habitual silence.

The two men at the table frowned and bristled:

"That ain't nothing, Gilbert," said one of them, "everybody in town knows all about that dynamite been missing. I heard it a week ago. They just found out who they think it is taday."

"It doesn't make any difference, Hyers," said Sam's father. "I don't want my son telling tales like that. It's none of his business to report what happens at the plant, especially when he doesn't work there, and hasn't any right to be hanging around there. You can't tell how soon something like that might get hanged on some kid that had nothing to do with it."

"I know," said Sam suddenly rousing to the conversation. "I heard Harry Wickers and Joe Landers found a stick of dynamite up in a field across the road from the plant, and they was throwing stones at it and trying to make it explode, and the night watchman at the plant just caught 'em in time, and stopped 'em. I think they oughtta tell all the kids how dangerous that is, don't you?"

The talk merged into a discussion of the rules about the plant and whether they were being carried out carefully, but Laurel heard no more. She was torturing herself with anxiety lest she had not done her duty with regard to what she had overheard on the porch and whether she ought to have reported it to someone at once.

She slept very little that night, and in the morning got up with the determination to write a letter to Phil Pilgrim and tell him all about it. She would ask him if there was someone up here she ought to tell, and ask him please to telegraph her at once. And then in the meantime, she must tell somebody here too if possible. Sam said Bruce Winter was looking after that dynamite, but somehow she didn't trust Bruce Winter. Was that silly? She might only be giving evidence to the wrong side by giving it to him, and yet, if he was in charge—!

There was more talk the next morning at the table about reporting rumors, and Sam's father gave him strict instructions not to tell *any*thing he heard outside the family.

One of the men brought down a radio from his room that night and turned on a speech about how people ought not to spread rumors, and ought to be very careful to find out if stories were officially confirmed before they told them anyway, and Sam wriggled around and at last came out with another story he had heard.

"They say there's more fifth column fellas in that

gang at the plant than they knew. They say they're doing all kinds of things to delay the work. They stop to tie their shoes, and then go and get drinks of water, and they get fits of coughing, and they pretend something's the matter with their machines. Anything to hold up the job."

"Look out, Sam, is that official?" asked his father in a severe tone.

"Yes, sir, it sure is, dad. I heard that there Winter they say is a top man telling some men as they came down to the village that it was so. He said he knew pretty well who had instigated it, but he wasn't arresting him yet. He wanted him to give himself away a little more before he fired him."

"Son, are you quite sure that was the man named Winter?" asked his father looking at Sam with a piercing glance.

"Well, I'm *mostly* sure," said Sam shifting his gaze to his plate. "He's the one Joe pointed out."

"Well, now, look here, Sam. You're '*mostly* sure,' that's all, and you're not *sure* at all. And even if you were you had no right to go and tell even your family what a big boss like you say he is said. He didn't say it for publication. That's just the kind of thing that is going to make it impossible to win the war if such things go on. And it seems to me a mighty queer thing for a big high up boss to go gossiping along the highway about, when he's supposed to be sworn to secrecy. It sounds kinda funny to me. A real man in an authoritative position would be sworn to keep such things to himself, or look out who he told them to. The man you heard talk might even be a fifth column man himself for all you know. So now I want it distinctly understood that *none* of my family go around telling anything that they have not seen themselves, and even then they might not have understood what it all meant. Do you understand, Sam?"

"Yes, sir!" said Sam with downcast eyes.

"Do you understand, Nannie?"

"Yes, Daddy," said Nannie lifting clear innocent eyes.

Laurel listened thoughtfully. She had all but decided to drive to the Price boarding house tonight and ask for Bruce Winter and tell him what she had overhead that night before he arrived. But this decided her. If Winter was as careless as that he wasn't trustworthy. Besides she wasn't at all sure that he was in such a responsible position as they seemed to think. She would wait another day. Perhaps she would still hear from Phil Pilgrim. If she didn't she would go to Mrs. Gray and ask her what wise man she should consult.

It was just then that someone rang the old-fashioned doorbell and Nannie brought in a telegram for Laurel.

Laurel excused herself and went to her room to read it. She found that she was trembling from head to foot, and she certainly did not want to be asked any questions just now.

Up in her room she locked her door and read the telegram.

> Message received. Have given the information to Brown, a man high in authority. He will call for you tomorrow afternoon at four P.M. at your school. You can trust him with all details. Letter follows airmail.
>
> Phil

Laurel sat for a minute or two in a daze. Why hadn't she done this before? Evidently the information she had given had been considered important enough for some officer to come and inquire into it. Well, she was glad it was going to be taken off her conscience. Would it be an ordeal to be questioned by an officer?

Then she began to try and plan for that interview.

Where could she hold it? Not at the school for the children would hang around and be curious. They would go home and report that she had had a visitor. And if he was a man in uniform they would get up all sorts of stories and proclaim them over the town. Word might even get to those men at the boarding house, and they would find out who had told about them. Also they would most effectually cover up their tracks so that she would be proved a fool, and that there was nothing to it all. She must somehow take him away where they could have privacy and nobody would overhear.

She couldn't bring him here to the house. There was no place to take a caller except the big dining room where any member of the household was liable to walk through at any moment and interrupt. There seemed no way to have privacy except to take him out in the car for a little drive. If it would only be fairly pleasant perhaps that would not be such a bad idea. Of course Phil would have told him enough to make him understand how she was situated.

She went over and over it, even to arranging the details of the story she had to tell, to make it as brief as possible, and yet get in every possible phase that could have any bearing on the case.

Then there would be the two young Gilberts whom she was in the habit of taking home every night when she left school. She would have to get rid of them on some pretext that would not make them suspicious. She decided to look after that on her way to school in the morning. So when Mrs. Frisbie was safely landed at her store for the day and she had turned her car toward the school she spoke.

"Sam! Nannie! I'm not going to be able to take you home today. I'm having a caller this afternoon, after school, and I'm taking him driving. I may not even be back in time for dinner, but you tell your mother not to bother saving anything for me if I'm not back on time. I'll get something on the way if I am late. Now, can I trust you to go right home and tell your mother that? And *not* tell *any*body else *any*thing unless they ask where I am, and then you can say I had a guest I took driving. If they ask you more just say you don't know. Can I trust you to do that for me? Please? Thank you! So don't wait for me, nor talk about this to *any* of the scholars."

They promised eagerly, glad to do anything she asked, and so the first worry was out of the way. She was sure Sam and Nannie would be absolutely mum about her affairs.

It was after they were out of the car, waiting for her to lock the door that Nannie said:

"But, Miss Sheridan. We're having *chicken* for supper tonight."

"Oh, I'm sorry, Nannie! That's just too bad for me, but I'll tell you what, if I'm late you and Sam divide my piece between you."

"No," said Nannie, "I'm sure Mom'll save it for you."

"Don't let her," said Laurel, and left them smiling.

The day seemed rushing on all too fast and Laurel was filled with forebodings as the hour for closing approached. But she sat quietly at her desk working over her class reports until the school was dismissed and had trooped away. Then a little interval, and at last she heard steps coming down the hall.

She looked up and there stood a man with keen pleasant eyes and a firm mouth. He was not in uniform.

"Is this Miss Sheridan?" he said crisply.

"Yes," said Laurel rising and gathering up her report cards to put in her desk.

"My name is Brown," said the man. "Is there some quiet place where we could talk a few minutes?"

"I thought perhaps we might take a drive in my car,"

said Laurel. "We would be rather liable to interruption either here or at my boarding place, I am afraid."

"Yes, I should suppose so. The car would be very good. Is it near here?"

"Just at the back of the school. Come this way."

Laurel had thought this out step by step, and had her wraps on a chair beside her. She put on her hat with one motion, and swept up her coat, handbag and gloves. The man followed her down the hall and out the back door. In a moment more they had turned into a side street and were riding away from Carrollton at a brisk pace.

"Now," said the stranger, "tell me please everything that happened, just when and where and how. I have of course seen your letter to Captain Pilgrim, and shall understand your references. The men's names are Byrger, Gratz and Schmidt. Is that right? And the other two whom you knew in the city are Winter and Rainey. Now if you will kindly give me details."

So Laurel began her story, driving slowly up the road where Adrian Faber had taken her that day several weeks ago, choosing that road because it did not go through town nor pass the homes of any of her pupils. She felt they would be all agog if they saw her with a strange man. The little village life was so cognizant and curious about every new happening.

So they drove on, the stranger interrupting now and then with a question. And when the story was told he said:

"Yes, I think I understand. And now, could we go through the town somehow and could you show me the boarding house, Crimson Mountain, the location of the plant, and any other places that seem important, especially that little cemetery lot, without making it too obvious?"

"I think so," said Laurel puckering her brows

thoughtfully, and trying to think quickly. "I'll do my best." They went speeding back to town, entering by side streets, and going around behind the old railroad siding at the Junction. Laurel tried to remember all that Pilgrim had told her about the roads that had never been so familiar to her in earlier days.

LAUREL had talked very quietly, and quickly. She had told the story just as she had thought it out in the waking hours of the night. She was sure she had not missed a detail.

The man beside her watched her as she talked, interpolated a keen question now and then, which Laurel answered as best she could, and sometimes could not answer. She saw at once that this man whom Phil Pilgrim had sent to her knew his business, and had no illusions about its being nothing but nonsense. He gave her assurance that the matter would be fully investigated. He told her that cases of this sort were his special business, and that she had been very wise in letting Pilgrim know what she had heard. He warned her not to tell anyone else. And then he began to question her about what she knew of Winter and Rainey, how she came to meet them, and what she knew of their history. Of course, though, she knew very little except the word that had currently gone about the city when they had been received freely in the circles where Adrian Faber moved.

"Oh, *Faber!*" said the stranger. "Yes, Faber. He's not a man who stops to find out very much about people he takes into his circle if they happen to please him socially. Didn't you find that so?"

Laurel looked thoughtful.

"Perhaps," she said hesitantly, surprised that he knew Adrian Faber. "I'm not sure. I never thought about that. I haven't known him so long. Perhaps you're right. I don't know who was responsible for bringing Mr. Winter and Mr. Rainey into the social circles, they just appeared one day and everybody accepted them as a matter of course. I heard they were former war correspondents from abroad. Germany perhaps. They claimed to be American born. But I heard yesterday that Mr. Winter is in charge of things up at the plant. Of course I don't know that that is true. I heard also that the two men, Gratz and Schmidt, have been arrested. It seems to be part of the rumors that are going around among the school children. I cannot vouch for it. Gratz and Schmidt are rather unpleasant looking men, very rough and uncouth. I only saw them a couple of times. The man I would be most likely to suspect is that strange, watchful, sullen man, with the gimlet eyes, Mr. Byrger. He's no American, I'm sure of that. He says he's an inventor and tries to give the impression he is making some mysterious secret up there that is going to win the war—for somebody! He doesn't say who."

"Yes?" said the visitor grimly, with that unbelieving rising inflection that creates immediate doubt in the mind of the listener.

It was then that they came to the two white headstones, gleaming there in the late afternoon sunshine, the roses long since dead and turned brown like the ground around them

Colonel Brown gave a quick glance around.

"Wait a minute!" he said. He got out of the car and

went over by the stone wall, giving a keen look over the place. His trained eyes saw disturbances in the ground that had been well camouflaged, but all he said when he came back to the car was, "Well, now, let's get on. The old Pilgrim house is next, isn't it? Across the road?"

He took out a diagram that Pilgrim had evidently drawn for him and studied it. He surveyed the sad drab home of the Pilgrims with grave eyes, scarcely pausing over it, and then they went on toward the road where the plant had been built. Laurel was surprised as she drew nearer the plant to see how amazingly large the building was, although it seemed such a short time since it was started. Six weeks they said such things were taking now, and being used even before they were entirely finished. They passed down the far road where they would not be seen by anybody working at the plant. Then whistles blew for changing shifts, and her companion gave the word to drive faster.

"There is a lower road here somewhere," he said. "It turns off to the right and goes around to Carrollton by way of the Junction. Pilgrim told me about it. We'd better go back that way. We'll be less likely to meet workmen returning for the night to their boarding places."

"Yes," said Laurel, and found herself following the old rough road up which she had come that first day to meet the cattle, and the man who saved her life.

Somehow it seemed as if this stranger were someone she had known long ago. His grave quiet manner put her at her ease. She wanted to ask him some questions, but she figured that it was not her business, and that just because she had happened on some evidence that was going to be valuable it did not give her the right to pry out other things.

But as they neared the station, where Colonel Brown had asked her to drop him for the train, she mustered courage to ask:

"Was Mr. Pilgrim well when you saw him?"

He turned to her with a lighting of his eyes.

"Yes," he said, "he is very well, and I had almost forgotten a most important commission he gave me. I was to give you greetings from him and best wishes. I also promised him that I would inform you that you have done a most important bit of detective work that may save the government much time and hard work to search out some of the people who are trying to undo us in favor of our enemies. Let me also say that I do appreciate the way you have helped me this afternoon. Do you anticipate that what you have done will cause you any annoyance or curious questioning from people who have no right to ask?"

"Oh, no," smiled Laurel. "I think not. We have met very few people I know, and they may not have even noticed that there was a stranger with me. I explained to the young people in whose home I board that I would have a caller this afternoon whom I was taking for a drive around to show the sights of the vicinity, and that I might not get home in time for dinner so they need not be worried. But now since you are leaving on that train I shall be home in plenty of time for the evening meal, and I shall not be subjected to questioning. The father of the family is very much opposed to his children telling any rumors they have heard, or asking any questions. He seems to have true breeding, although he is a poor, hard-working man. So I shall just go in as usual, and nothing will happen I am sure. But you don't know how relieved I am to have this matter off my mind. I have been so worried lest I ought to do something, and didn't know what to do."

"Well, you certainly did the right thing, and selected the best man you could have found to confide in. Not only because he has rare good sense and is a man to be trusted utterly, but also because he knows this place, this situation, and can advise, as well as pass on information. He is a valuable man and I suspect is in line for promotion soon."

"Oh," said Laurel with a catch in her voice, "does that mean that he will be sent far away—perhaps overseas?"

Brown smiled.

"Of course I have no authority to make positive statements but I should say not. He is too valuable a man to waste that way. We need him right here. His technical training has been very fine and will be worth a great deal in defense work. He is a mechanical genius and it doesn't take the government long to discover people like that!"

Laurel's eyes were shining now. She loved to hear Phil Pilgrim praised, and her heart rejoiced over the possibility that he might not have to go overseas.

"Thank you for telling me that!" she said, her face aglow.

"And there is one other thing I'd like to say, before I leave you, and that is that I think Phil Pilgrim knows how to select his friends, if I may judge by the one I have been with this afternoon. I do hope I have not imposed upon your time too much, and I shall be glad to have you call upon me at any time if there should arise an occasion where I could help you in any way. You certainly have rendered efficient help today. Now, it's about time for my train and I guess I'd better get out and say good-by. I hope I shall see you again!"

When he was gone Laurel sat thoughtfully a minute or two before she started her car for home. What a pleasant experience it had been. It was almost like seeing Pilgrim again to meet someone who admired him so much!

Then she went smiling back to the house, put up her

car, and went up to her room, stopping in the dining room only long enough to call to Mrs. Gilbert that she was home and hungry as a bear for that chicken dinner she had heard about.

It was hard for her to bring her thoughts down to study that evening, because there were so many things to think about, and her face was very happy when she went down to dinner.

"You had a good time, didn't you?" whispered Nannie happily. "I'm glad. I *like* you to be happy."

"You dear child!" she said as she went over to her chair, reflecting about this dear plain family in which she was living, whom she was growing to love, and who were beginning to love her. Could anything be better than that? It made up for all lack of service and luxury. She was glad she had come here. She wanted to stay here as long as she stayed in this town, if they would let her, and she saw by the light in all their faces that they wanted her.

She ate the delicious supper and enjoyed every bite. The tender chicken that had been simmering all the afternoon. The delicate dumplings, rows and rows of them around the big generous platter, in the sea of delicious gravy. Could anybody have a better supper? Little white onions that had been growing on the garden lot behind the house, creamed now, and sweet as honey. Delightful pickles that had come out of Mother Gilbert's big kettle that very fall, made from tender little cucumbers grown in that same garden. Fluffy white potatoes, also garden products. If that same dinner were being served in a grand hotel or some fine restaurant it would be at a fabulous price. This simple boarding house where things were crude, and cheap, had yet the most delicious food that Laurel had ever tasted. Not fancy, but very fine and wholesome and delicious. Oh, she wouldn't go back to Mrs. Price's house, not even if she had it all to herself.

Later in the evening Mrs. Gilbert talked about how pleased they were to have her with them.

"My man has made up his mind that we are doing wrong to give up our parlor to board another man. He says we are to put the things back. He doesn't like it that we have no place for us to gather after supper. He says you, a real lady, have no place to take your friends when they come to see you, so you have to take them out to ride."

"Oh, my dear!" said Laurel, "I don't need a parlor. I seldom will have visitors. This man who came today was only bringing me a message from a dear friend of mine, and had to go on his way by the afternoon train. You must not feel you have to give up a room that you could use for another one or two boarders. Please, I wouldn't like to feel that I had done that to you. I would feel I had to go away if I were hampering you in what you felt you ought to do."

"No!" said Mrs. Gilbert. "You are not hampering us. Pop feels the children have a right to a parlor. He didn't like it after we took the parlor things out and put them in the loft of the barn. He's going to bring them back tonight. And what's more he says you haven't got a fitting room for a real lady like you. We want you should take the big room over the parlor. The children are there now, but we got them places fixed and they want *you* to have the big room."

"Oh, but Mrs. Gilbert. I wouldn't give up my little room for anything!" said Laurel. "I *love* it! Why you don't know how I feel about my view of Crimson Mountain. I wouldn't give that up for anything. No, don't tell me the next room has the same view. It *hasn't!* I tried it the other day, and I couldn't see the same trees.

I want to stay right where I am if you please. You may fix your parlor if you feel you want it for yourselves, but I'm perfectly satisfied without one."

"Well, my dear, then we want it for ourselves, if you'd rather we put it that way."

So they settled it at last, and Laurel went up to her room and lay down on her hard little cot, looking out on old Crimson, watching till the moon went down like a great gold piece and old Crimson was dark, save for those watchlights about the plant. She smiled in the darkness as she thought of her beloved who had first shown her the heart of Crimson Mountain, who had made her see the story of his hard young life, just by pointing to an old gray farmhouse, and two gleaming white headstones. She felt so close to him tonight, because the man who admired and trusted him had been with her. She lay there thinking over all that he had said about Phil Pilgrim, and wondering if his predictions would really come true. Her heart throbbed with a sweet thrill and she realized how she loved him. How short a time she had known him as measured by the calendar, but how sure she was that he was all she believed.

She no longer worried now about that plant with its dynamite and the two quiet graves. She had put the whole matter into the hands of that quiet man who had taken over, and she need not think of it any more. Something would be done by the government, if it really needed doing.

So the days went by and everything went calmly on. Mrs. Frisbie and Mrs. Gilbert were attending the Tuesday Bible classes now, and loved it. Mrs. Gray had been to call on them, and loved them, Laurel was beginning to feel that she had a very nice circle of friends, although to tell the truth, they were not many of them her age, unless she could count the adoring Nannie and the devoted Sam. She had almost forgotten Adrian Faber and the gay crowd who followed him.

And then one night at supper, after an exciting day in which rumors ran riot that more dynamite had been stolen, one of the men boarders who worked in the plant reported they had finished their first consignment of work. It was a lot of queer gadgets that belonged to the much discussed "mysterious invention" which was going to do something great for aviation. They were ready for shipment to the plant that was making the planes they were to complete.

Then the next morning Sam came back to breakfast from his morning route and announced that the government was sending a special detachment from the army to protect the plant on Crimson Mountain. He said that the three old farmhouses in the region of the plant were to be used for barracks for the army men, and they were to stay up there and look after things. This announcement was of such importance that even Mr. Gilbert couldn't object to its being told so Sam had full freedom for the time to report all he knew. It was a great thing that real soldiers were to be established on their mountain and the town began to take on importance.

Laurel wondered, and pondered and prayed about it, but she said not a word of course to anybody about the momentous visit of Colonel Brown, nor whether his visit had had anything to do with placing the soldiers there, but she couldn't help thinking that it had.

Laurel liked to think there were soldiers on her mountain. She hoped they would protect the graves of the two old people who were so dear to Phil Pilgrim. She wondered if the soldiers would be told about those graves and the discovery that they had been used as a place of concealment for stolen explosives. Then she wondered who those soldiers were. Probably very young men who had to be put through an easy job before going into more serious war work. Yet, if the things they were making in the plant were important, and a secret, it seemed as if the people who protected them should be people who understood the seriousness of the business.

Laurel was getting quite in the habit of making old Crimson a sort of confidante at night, after she had retired, and thinking a lot about Pilgrim too. He hadn't written much since the Colonel's visit. Just brief notes saying how busy he was, and that things were still uncertain for him yet, though he thought he would be moving soon.

Late one afternoon Laurel was at the garage getting her car serviced for morning, when she saw a bunch of men coming down the road from the plant. Winter was marching ahead of them talking angrily to the man behind him.

She slid back as far as she could behind the wheel and was diligently studying a road map as the men came by and they did not seem to notice her, but she could hear every word they said. She had had one or two just such narrow escapes in near-meeting Winter, but so far he hadn't recognized her.

"Yes, and do you know who they've put in charge of the most important part of the plant? Over *us*, mind you! Over *me* the *manager!* They've put a young guy in uniform! Imagine that! He probably wouldn't know the front end of a machine even if you gave him lessons. I'm going to send in a protest. Dexter ought to know about this. I intend to see that he gets a complaint. And it's time those soldiers had a little lesson in keeping out of the way. He'll get his, you'll see, and I don't mean maybe."

They passed on and again Laurel had that feeling of distrust. How could you tell just by a voice whether you could trust a man or not?

And after them came Byrger, his little gimlet eyes hurrying from side to side, watching all ways at once, a sly look in them, a cringing attitude, a look of hate and belligerence on his narrow face. She drew farther back in her car, turning her face away from him. He must not see her now. She felt a great dislike for him. Why was it? Just because she had heard him talk that night in the boarding house?

And then as they turned into the village street she noticed that Winter and Rainey drew near together talking earnestly, and casting black looks back toward Byrger.

That evening in her room Laurel looked at Old Crimson. It had lost its garland of yellow leaves at last and taken on wintry look. Little gray twigs made a gray lace pattern against a wintry sky, and the mountain top had that barren look that comes when decorations are gone. Laurel looked out sadly at it and thought of those young soldiers up there in a strange place, in the cold and dark, boys from nice homes probably, and not in the least interested in the gadgets they were protecting. She sighed however with relief to know they were there. Would she ever see any of them at all?

And then she fell asleep.

She was awakened roughly by a tremendous explosion, so loud it seemed that all the foundations of the earth had been rent asunder, and cast up into the air. It shook the house and the bed on which she lay, and brought her upright staring straight ahead of her. Was that an earthquake?

And then there were more explosions, and a sound of rending rocks, shattered window-glass, falling debris. Looking up she saw a crimson glow in her room, lighting the walls. Crimson Mountain itself seemed to be burning! Just as she had dreamed in her imagination that it would do, so it seemed to be on fire. A great red flame shot up to heaven, showing all the fine sharp branches of the old bare mountain trees that had borne such glowing foliage just a little while before. It flared and spread, trickling in hungry tongues of flame down the mountain side.

The glare lit up the heavens from one end of the sky to the other. And now she could see figures up there, running back and forth, and she could hear shoutings, and screams and groans. Had the great plant been blown up? Had anything happened to the secret gadgets that had been made and were to have been sent out today to begin their work in the war? Was this sabotage? And where were the soldiers? Were any of them hurt? And now the fire engines from Carrollton, and other nearby towns, began to arrive, and the people of the town arose and went to the rescue of Crimson Mountain.

THE morning went on, but the whole town was filled with excitement. So many homes had men working in the plant, and as yet so little was known of the result of the disaster. Rumors kept drifting down from Crimson, of this one and that one hurt or killed, but no one knew anything as yet.

Laurel, white and shaken, went to school, but there were so few children there that it seemed useless to try to carry on the classes. At noon the superintendent dismissed the school for the day. None of the older boys had even come. They were all up on Crimson Mountain helping to put out the fire, helping to rescue injured men and get them to the hospital, caring for the dead and dying.

One of the first reports that came down from the mountain was that some of the soldiers had been killed, and some were missing. But no one knew anything definitely, and because she had a soldier of her own Laurel was full of sorrow for the people who loved these young soldiers.

Then there came more definite word. The man

Winter had been killed. Rainey was badly burned. They were not sure he would live. Byrger had not been found yet. In all they reported twelve men dead, and more missing, or badly injured, but the count was not all in yet.

Sam came rushing home early in the afternoon, blackened almost beyond recognition, calling for food. He wanted some sandwiches, too, for the boys who were working with him. And while he was eating and his mother and Nannie and Laurel were making sandwiches as fast as their fingers could fly, he talked:

"Say, who d'ya think is up there in charge of those soldiers, moms? Phil Pilgrim, moms, *our* Phil Pilgrim that useta work at the old filling station, and useta come here sometimes and talk ta dad. *Our* Phil Pilgrim! And he's a captain now. Captain Pilgrim. I heard 'em say it. I saw him once, not very near though. He was carrying that man Winter to the ambulance;—Winter is dead ya know. But I guess Phil Pilgrim must a been burned ur something. He had a rag around his arm and it was all blood. They say he was in charge of the plant since he came, and it was through him those things they been making in such a hurry to ship away got saved. Whoever did this thing was figuring to finish the works, sabotage ya know. They think it was Byrger, or mebbe Winter too, and they double-crossed each other, for Winter is dead, and Byrger is gone. So they think Byrger did it, and then beat it. Rainey's unconscious so they can't ask him if he knows. But anyhow Phil Pil—*Captain* Pilgrim I mean—when he got up there after the men had gone home to supper, he ordered his men to take those big boxes out of the building—you see the things were all packed for shipment and in the building where they were made, and he had 'em taken out and placed where they could be picked up early in the morning when the trucks came by on the road, and so he saved them. They didn't mean they should be saved, but *he saved* 'em. *Some* said he went in where the fire was still burning, as soon as the explosions stopped and pulled the last of the boxes out himself at the risk of his life, and that's how he got burned, but nobody seems to really know. But anyhow he saved the stuff. And, moms, can't I bring him home to dinner if he can get off?"

White faced, Laurel listened to the tale. Phil Pilgrim *here?* Phil Pilgrim up in that terrible fiery furnace! Oh, dear God! And he was alive yet and safe? Oh, if she could but go to him and find out.

Sam was off with what sandwiches they had had time to make, and then Mrs. Gilbert sent the children to the store for more bread and butter and canned meat and eggs, and set them all to work.

"We'll make some more sandwiches," she said with a sad little smile. "There'll be others hungry too."

So they worked nearly all the afternoon, sending Nannie and the boys half way up the mountain with the basket, where Sam was to be on the lookout for them.

Laurel, while she worked, was praying.

About the middle of the afternoon Mrs. Gray came walking over. She had been making sandwiches too, and put hers in with theirs.

"I'm so glad you're all right," she said to Laurel. "You seem so near to the mountain over here I was afraid your house would suffer. Only two windows broken! That's wonderful! And have you heard anything definite about the soldiers? I am told that Phil Pilgrim was in charge of them. Is that so?"

"Oh, I don't know anything more than Sam told us. We haven't heard again," and Laurel repeated what Sam had said.

There were tears in Mrs. Gray's eyes as she listened.

"Oh, but we'll be praying for Phil," she said softly. "He is the Lord's own. I'm sure he'll be cared for!"

It seemed as if that afternoon stretched out to age-long lengths after Laurel heard that Pilgrim was on Crimson Mountain. Her soul was tortured with questions which could not be answered. But she found her comfort in letting her heart cry out softly to God.

They were just sitting down to a hastily cooked supper when the men began to come home.

"There's dad!" said Sam. "I guess he's good and tired. He'll wantta wash before he eats. Some of you children take him up some warm water."

Then the men who worked in the plant began to come. They were good conscientious men who had stuck by the work when the explosion came. One of them was badly burned and had been taken to the hospital, two of them had been on night duty, but all had been working all day. They did not say much. They were grave and sad and silent. One cannot be as near as they had been to horror like that inferno without having a changed attitude toward life.

And then, while they were all eating, and Sam was explaining why he didn't bring Phil Pilgrim home to supper, the doorbell rang.

"I couldn't find him," Sam said. "Some said he had gone up where the fire was still burning to see if he could find any more bodies, but that was beyond the line where they would let us boys go, so all I could do was to send him a message by Pete Rafferty. He was going up there, and he said he'd give it. I told him you all wanted him to come to supper, no matter how late!"

Laurel got up quickly from the table.

"I'll go to the door," she said. She wanted a chance to get her breath after hearing that Pilgrim had gone up to where the fire was still burning.

But one of the little girls got up and opened the dining room door into the hall, so she could see who was at the door.

Laurel opened the door slowly, after taking a deep breath and preparing herself for anything that might be waiting for her behind that door. And there stood Pilgrim!

She looked at him for an instant, and then her face bloomed into joy.

"Oh, my *dear!*" she said and there were sudden tears of joy in her eyes, "are—you—all right?" There was almost a sob in her voice as she spoke.

And Phil Pilgrim, black and grimed and disheveled, one sleeve torn away, one bloody shirt sleeve showing, a look of utter weariness and sudden joy upon his young face, gazed down on her as if it were the greatest sight he had ever looked upon. Then he put his arms out and gathered Laurel into them, and stooped and kissed her, long and sweet upon her lips, holding her close to that torn, wet, dirty uniform, and it seemed to her the dearest place she had ever been in her life.

"It's Phil Pilgrim!" announced Nannie in the most sibilant of whispers that the whole table could hear.

"Yes, it's Phil Pilgrim," said the little sister Daisy with wide astonished eyes, "and he *kissed* our Laurel Sheridan! Does he *know* our Laurel?"

"Yes, it's Phil Pilgrim of course," proclaimed Sam triumphantly. "Didn't I tell ya he was coming? Who else would it be I'd like ta know?"

"But—he—*kissed*—our Laurel Sheridan, right on her *mouth* he kissed her!" objected the littlest sister. "I *saw* him! Moms, that isn't nice, is it?"

But nobody was paying attention to her now, everybody was up and coming toward the door, and there stood that tired dirty soldier with his dear girl in his arms, and a look of Heaven in his face.

They gave the guest a chance to wash his hands and face, and then they brought him to the table and gave him of their best, while Laurel sat beside him and waited on him. And when at last the room was quiet for an instant, little Daisy who had not taken her eyes off the two while they were in the room, found voice again:

"But, moms, you always told me it wasn't *nice* for girls to let boys kiss them. Not on their *mouths*. And not *any*way if they didn't *know* each other!"

Then there was a loud roar of laughter from the entire table, and Daisy puckered her lip, looked around the table in dismay, and then burst into tears, with great big heart-wrung sobs.

It took some time for Daisy to be quieted, but finally when Phil Pilgrim took her on his lap and began to talk to her gently she stopped crying and began to smile.

"But you see, little sister," he said, quite clearly so they all could hear, "I *do* know your Laurel Sheridan. In fact we're quite old friends," and he gave Laurel a quick merry wink. "And Daisy, we're going to be something *better* than friends some day pretty soon."

"Oh!" said Daisy. "Is there something better than friends?"

"Yes," said Pilgrim solemnly, "there's something better than friends. Some day pretty soon I hope, we are going to be married!"

Daisy looked from one to the other of them for a minute uncertainly, and then her face broke into smiles.

"Oh!" she said joyously. "I guess that is nice. Can I be bridesmaid?"

"Well, we'll have to talk that over and see," said Pilgrim. "Those details are not all settled yet. Perhaps you might be flower girl or something."

"Oh," said Daisy, "what is a detail? Could I be one of those too? Will it be tomorrow? Because my white dress isn't ironed yet."

"No, probably not tomorrow," said Pilgrim. "I have to do a little cleaning up on Crimson Mountain first you know and you'll have time to iron your dress. And now, suppose you hop down, little detail, and go and finish your dinner. I've got to finish mine and get back to my job pretty soon."

So Daisy reluctantly hopped down and went to her neglected plate and they all began to eat again, Laurel with her cheeks quite rosy, and one hand in Pilgrim's under the edge of the tablecloth.

When supper was finished they opened the parlor door. Dad had supervised the putting back of the old furniture into the parlor and now there was a suitable place for the lovers to go, when the rest of the family at the instigation of the mother, all drifted away to duties.

So they sat down on the old haircloth sofa, and had a blessed few minutes together.

Pilgrim brought out a little box from an inner pocket.

"This is yours, my dear, if you will have it," he said, looking down at the box, and then up to Laurel's lovely face. "It was my dear mother's engagement ring. She gave it to me when she was dying. I've carried it over my heart ever since. Perhaps it's a bit old-fashioned now, but I wanted to give it to you because it's all I have yet. Will you like it or would you rather I waited till I can get you a better one, a diamond?"

Laurel looked down at the ring as he slipped it on her finger.

"Oh, I would rather have this one. I shall love it. Why, Phil, it's a star sapphire! A lovely one. I've always wanted to have a star sapphire. And I shall like it so much better because it was your mother's!"

He gathered her close and their lips met once more. It seemed the sweetest moment of their lives.

And then suddenly the old parlor door swung softly open and there stood Daisy wide-eyed and wondering.

They looked up smiling, and then a scared expression

came over her face. She turned and fled toward the dining room, calling in a loud startled voice:

"Moms! They're doing it again! They're kissing each other again. What do they wantta do that for?"

"Sh-ss-sh!"

About the Author

Grace Livingston Hill is well-known as one of the most prolific writers of romantic fiction. Her personal life was fraught with joys and sorrows not unlike those experienced by many of her fictional heroines.

Born in Wellsville, New York, Grace nearly died during the first hours of life. But her loving parents and friends turned to God in prayer. She survived miraculously, thus her thankful father named her Grace.

Grace was always close to her father, a Presbyterian minister, and her mother, a published writer. It was from them that she learned the art of storytelling. When Grace was twelve, a close aunt surprised her with a hardbound, illustrated copy of one of Grace's stories. This was the beginning of Grace's journey into being a published author.

In 1892 Grace married Fred Hill, a young minister, and they soon had two lovely young daughters. Then came 1901, a difficult year for Grace—the year when, within months of each other, both her father and husband died. Suddenly Grace had to find a new place to live (her home was owned by the church where her husband had been pastor). It was a struggle for Grace to raise her young daughters alone, but through everything she kept writing. In 1902 she produced *The Angel of His Presence*, *The Story of a Whim*, and *An Unwilling Guest*. In 1903 her two books *According to the Pattern* and *Because of Stephen* were published.

It wasn't long before Grace was a well-known author, but she wanted to go beyond just entertaining her readers. She soon included the message of God's salvation through Jesus Christ in each of her books. For Grace, the most important thing she did was not write books but share the message of salvation, a message she felt God wanted her to share through the abilities he had given her.

In all, Grace Livingston Hill wrote more than one hundred books, all of which have sold thousands of copies and have touched the lives of readers around the world with their message of "enduring love" and the true way to lasting happiness: a relationship with God through his Son, Jesus Christ.

In an interview shortly before her death, Grace's devotion to her Lord still shone clear. She commented that whatever she had accomplished had been God's doing. She was only his servant, one who had tried to follow his teaching in all her thoughts and writing.